THE POWER OF
P.A.C.T. IN

ATTRACTING
AUTHENTIC
RELATIONSHIPS

THE POWER OF
P.A.C.T. IN

ATTRACTING
AUTHENTIC
RELATIONSHIPS

The Guide to Being Emotionally Safe,
Connected, and Successful
in Personal and Professional Relationships

RICO ARMSTRONG

The Power Of P.A.C.T. in Attracting Authentic Relationships: The Guide to Being Emotionally Safe, Connected, and Successful in Personal and Professional Relationships
Copyright © 2025 by Rico Armstrong

Published in Dallas, Texas, by Let's Go! Press

ISBN 979-8-9986107-0-7 (paperback)

Library of Congress Control Number: 2025907161

Printed in The United States
10 9 8 7 6 5 4 3 2 1

Contents

Prelude   **ix**

Introduction   **xi**

PART ONE: Awakening to Self-Awareness   **1**

   1   How Did We Get Here?   **3**

PART TWO: The P.A.C.T. Method: How Relationships Work **15**

   2   Understanding P.A.C.T. in Relationships **17**

   3   Purpose: Your Core Driver   **27**

   4   Authenticity: Beyond the Surface **41**

   5   Communication: The Bridge to Connection **51**

   6   Trust: The Foundation   **59**

Contents

PART THREE: Toxic vs. Attractive Communication   **67**

  7   Communication: The Language of Connection   **69**

  8   Toxic Communication: The Language of
Unhealthy Relationships   **77**

  9   Judgment: Closing Minds, Connection, and Collaboration   **83**

 10   Shame: The Trust Destroyer   **91**

 11   The Cost of Toxic Communication
and How to Break Free   **97**

 12   Attractive Communication and the 3 C's   **105**

 13   Lead With Curiosity: Opening Minds and Hearts   **109**

 14   Changing Misunderstandings to Understanding   **119**

 15   Courtesy and Tact: Say What You Mean
Without Being Mean   **127**

PART FOUR: Your Communication Transformation   **135**

 16   The Secret Fourth C: Charisma   **137**

 17   Mastering Vocal Tone: The Hidden Key to Influence   **145**

Contents

PART FIVE: Building Trust and Aligning Values   **157**

18   Your Purpose, Values, and the Circle of Trust   **159**

19   Breaking Free from the Past   **177**

20   Creating Healthy Boundaries: Protecting Your
      Circle of Trust   **193**

21   How to Communicate with a Narcissist   **203**

PART SIX: Applying P.A.C.T. In Real World Scenarios   **213**

22   The Art of First Impressions   **215**

23   Influential Leadership: Stand Out in Your Career   **225**

PART SEVEN: Your Relationship Transformation   **233**

24   Choose Your Relationships Wisely   **235**

25   The Joy of Quality Connections   **245**

Glossary   **251**

Diagrams and Illustrations   **253**

Recommended Reading   **257**

About the Author   **259**

Prelude

Forming relationships that make you feel emotionally safe—relationships that inspire both you and others to achieve your dreams—has become increasingly elusive for many. What if the key to meaningful connections isn't as complicated as it's often made out to be? I've encountered more than my fair share of relationship advice that only led to confusion and heartache. The result? Decades of hard-earned lessons learned the painful way. I used to wish for a guide, a mentor, someone who could share principles of relationships and communication grounded in wisdom, experience, and research—not just opinion. This book is that guide—the one I wish I had earlier in life. It's here to offer you what I didn't have, with the hope that you can bypass some of the pain and confusion I experienced and build better relationships from the start.

This book is not simply about taking personal experience and projecting it to you, as if to imply: "I figured it out all by my wise and all-knowing self and abilities." Instead, this book is the culmination of wisdom from over 40 books from leading experts, scientists, and researchers. I demonstrate how their work has impacted my life and the lives of others, along with practical examples of how to apply their concepts in real-world situations. This book distills the core principles from all this information into a simple, memorable framework that you can quickly apply in any situation.

There is no magic script for influence or authentic connection. Words are not magic like Harry Potter spells with one best "spell" for a specific result. However, words that are applied through principles allow you to be flexible in how you attract and influence authentic connections in ever-changing situations. While this book offers suggestions on specific ways to say things, its primary focus is more about teaching you principles of relationships and communication and how to apply them.

In closing, I want to ask you a question…have you ever read a non-fiction book and thought, "I wish this chapter and the stories in it were much longer?" I have never said that either. This book intends to keep the chapters short and pithy so you remember the points more clearly and apply them quickly. Here's to your success in attracting and maintaining the best relationships in your life!

Introduction

The day my father ghosted me was the day I started to question if I was a likable, lovable human. I was just nine years old. My parents divorced when I was two, and I lived with my mother. Every other weekend, my father would pick me up, and I'd look forward to the time we'd spend together. Spending time with him was fun, and I always learned something from him! As a young boy, I eagerly anticipated his visits, my heart filling with excitement at the thought of seeing him.

But sometimes, he would cancel our plans. As disappointing as it was, at least he would give me a few days' notice. Until one time, he didn't. He simply didn't show up. No phone call. No explanation. He just disappeared. Little did I know, that would be the last time I'd see him during my childhood years.

What if I told you that 70% of people have experienced emotional trauma or abuse at least once in their lives? What if 25% of those individuals are children 16 years or younger? If you've experienced emotional trauma—whether through neglect, abandonment, verbal abuse, or toxic relationships—chances are, it has affected your future relationships, both personal and professional.

At a young age, I became part of those statistics. I experienced emotional abandonment. And when my mother died when I was just 14, I felt abandoned all over again. These experiences, along with others, led to decades of struggles with self-esteem, toxic relationships, and trust issues. If you've faced similar struggles, there's a strong possibility you too have experienced emotional trauma in one or more of your relationships.

Relationships are at the heart of everything we do, yet mastering the art of communication and connection often feels like an elusive goal. We're told to "just be nice" or "be yourself," but these vague platitudes offer little practical guidance and, depending on your life experience, are easier said than done. On the other hand, it's easy to be overwhelmed with a sea of communication and relationship advice, making it challenging to know where to start or how to make sense of it all.

This is where "Choose Your P.A.C.T." comes in. This book is designed to help you develop authentic, trusting, and emotionally safe relationships with the people who matter most—both personally and professionally. No more guessing about how to build or attract the best relationships with a romantic partner, or how to gain the trust of your workmates. No more toxic situationships, marriages, or work environments. No more letting past experiences of emotional trauma or abuse affect your current or future relationships. Most importantly, no more self-doubt or masking insecurities. You will gain higher self-esteem, greater confidence, and have a positive influence on your life and those around you.

This book offers a powerful framework that distills the essence of all communication and relationship advice into a single, cohesive filter. As you continue your journey of personal growth, this framework will allow you to easily process and apply even the most nuanced insights you encounter *(see page 257 for a list of content that influences the framework in this book).*

Our approach is intentionally practical and experience-driven. Rather than bogging you down with academic rhetoric, we get straight to the point, using real-life stories to illustrate powerful principles. These narratives, some drawn from my own experiences and others (with names and details altered to protect privacy), showcase tools forged in the fire of real-world challenges and triumphs.

At the core of this book lies a profound and fundamental truth: the better you understand yourself, the better you can understand others. And the better you understand others, the more effectively you can communicate with them. This journey of self-discovery requires vulnerability and courage. Only by honestly exploring your inner world can you articulate your life's purpose and begin to heal any emotional trauma that may be blocking your ability to connect deeply with others or align with your true calling.

P.A.C.T., introduced in this book, is built on four key pillars:

- **Purpose:** Aligning your values and goals
- **Authenticity:** Character-based qualities that draw others to you
- **Communication:** The art of clear, empathetic exchange
- **Trust:** Building mutual reliability and emotional safety

Through this lens, you'll gain insights into:

- Recognizing and avoiding toxic communication patterns
- Developing charisma and influential leadership skills
- Setting healthy boundaries without damaging relationships
- Navigating difficult conversations with confidence
- Creating lasting personal and professional connections

Whether you're looking to deepen existing relationships, forge new ones, or simply become a more effective communicator, the principles in this book will serve as your guide. By the time you finish reading, you'll have a clear understanding of what makes relationships work, why they sometimes fail, and how to cultivate connections that truly enrich your life.

Let's begin this journey towards mastering the art of human connection, armed with a framework that will serve you for years to come.

PART ONE

Awakening to Self-Awareness

Every transformative journey begins with self-awareness. In this section, we'll explore a powerful story of awakening, paired with foundational research that highlights the profound impact of relationships. Through this personal story and scientific insights, you'll begin to reflect on how your past experiences shape your approach to connection, and why understanding yourself is the first critical step in mastering meaningful relationships. This section is about understanding the deep human drive to connect, belong, and grow together.

How Did We Get Here?

Having a gun pointed at you should be terrifying. But as I sat there, all I felt was peace. That's when I knew something was terribly wrong, worse than I realized. How had I gotten to this point?...

At 36, I met an incredible woman who seemed like the perfect life partner. She was amazing with kids, a driven professional, and deeply passionate about her health. I envisioned us as a power couple—great parents, unwavering supporters of each other's dreams, and that effortlessly cool older couple who "still got it" as we grew old together. We got married in April.

Two years later, I started to question the value of my life. By this point, my personal and professional life was dismal. I was not talking to my friends, and they were not talking to me. I isolated myself. I left the fitness career I loved for a corporate job that I hated.

Additionally, every time I tried to pursue something more in line with my purpose, my wife told me that I was irresponsible, my ideas would never work, and she would not support my efforts to work towards my purpose.

Six months after that, in March, right around my birthday. I was seriously considering ending my life. This thought, and the accompanying feelings, came as a big surprise to me. In hindsight, it should not have been. Yet, it still was.

I knew I had to get a new perspective on my life, and fast.

My entire journey had been built on understanding human connection - and now, ironically, it was this very connection that was missing. What I discovered and experienced next would change everything I thought I knew about relationships.

The Research Behind Relationships

Before this moment, I had come to a strong belief: The quality of your relationships is the most powerful influence on your health, wealth, and overall well-being. THE RIGHT connection with the right people can change everything.

After developing this belief, I discovered this is backed by the longest-running research study ever—the Harvard Study of Adult Development (formerly known as The Grant Study) started in 1938. Scientists began tracking the health of 268 Harvard sophomores during the Great Depression. The study expanded to 1300 people, including the offspring of the 268 candidates. In addition to studying their health, they also studied the success and/or failures of their careers and marriages.

Here's the startling truth revealed by a well-researched and documented study:

> *"Loneliness kills. It's as powerful as smoking or alcoholism… The surprising finding is that our relationships and how happy we are in our relationships have a powerful influence on our health. Taking care of your body is important, but tending to your relationships is a form of self-care too."*
> -Robert Waldinger, Professor of Psychiatry, Harvard Medical School

In summary, this study concluded that the quality of our relationships predicts our health, wealth, and happiness more accurately than diet, exercise routine, or career.

How We Got Here

While the Harvard study validated my beliefs about relationships, I was living proof of the harm they can also cause — their darker side. I was not in a good place mentally, and I was struggling to find a reason to keep going. It was literally killing me.

Once I recognized the severity of my emotional and mental state, I did what felt natural — I turned to my wife, my life partner. I opened up to her, sharing my deepest thoughts and feelings without holding anything back. She graciously listened without judgment, and I was grateful for that.

- I told her I felt alone in and out of the house.
- I told her how working the job I hated was affecting me.
- I expressed how disheartening it was not pursuing my purpose, and how overwhelmingly guilty I felt for being a husband who so often seems to be disappointing his wife, despite his best efforts.
- I told her I was grieving the fact that I was currently not the happy, energetic, fit person I was just 2 years ago (I gained some weight by this point).

It was one of the hardest, most vulnerable conversations of my life. I wasn't looking for her to fix me — I knew that wasn't her job. But I did hope she might meet me in my pain, or at the very least, grab my hand and help me figure out where to go from there. I thought that's what life partners did when one of them was drowning.

Her response was not what I expected. She did not shame me or judge me for expressing myself. Thank goodness for that! But what she did say was alarming and shocking. Without harshness or malice, she simply said something to the effect of: *"You are going to have to figure your shit out on your own. I do not know how to help you, and I'm not going to try and figure out how to."*

I froze. Did I hear her right? My mind scrambled to process what she had just said. Part of me hoped she'd follow it up with, *"But I'm here for you"* or *"Let's figure it out together"* — but she didn't. She firmly held her position, leaving me sitting there in my pain with no lifeline.

It crushed me. I don't say this to make her the villain of my story — but I won't pretend that her response didn't sting deeply. When the person you love the most, the person you share a life with, essentially says, *"You're on your own with this,"* it's hard not to feel abandoned. I didn't expect her to have all the answers, but I did expect her to *care enough to try.*

Not long after that, I had my life threatened. On Interstate 30 in Dallas, TX, a man in a white van speeds past me on the narrow shoulder lane going 100 miles per hour cutting me off. Suddenly, as we both exit, he comes to a complete stop. I slam on the brakes, but there is not enough space between us. I lightly tap his back bumper. As I u-turn under the highway overpass to pull over, he speeds up again. This time, he pulls around to the side of my car and points his gun at me. I slam my brakes. He pulls over about one-eighth of a mile ahead, just between me and the on-ramp to the highway. I can't drive by him. I'm stuck.

The Breaking Point

Having a gun pointed at you for the first time in your life (or perhaps anytime ever) should be terrifying. But as I sat there, all

I felt was peace. It was one of those moments when time slowed down. I was not afraid, not even a little bit.

I remember thinking, "If this is how my life ends, this might be the best way possible. Death will be quick. My life insurance will take care of my wife and parents. I will not suffer anymore. I will not disappoint myself and my wife anymore…" When someone presents an opportunity to take your life so you don't have to do it yourself, especially when you're at the height of losing the will to live, the chance seems almost too perfect.

Fortunately, my mother said something to me as a child that created what I now call a 'Fail Safe.'" For me, this Fail Safe is a belief that protects from purposeful self-harm and makes it very difficult to carry out suicidal thoughts. In a moment of vulnerability as a struggling single parent, my mother says to me: "Son, the only reason I'm alive some days is for you." I was 10 years old when she told me this. Those words were sobering, heavy, and unforgettable. Interestingly, those words would shape and instill a belief in me, a Fail-Safe, that may very well have saved my life!

Those words my mother said solidified a belief in my mind: "Suicide is a selfish act." At that moment, rationalizing suicide wasn't just unfair to me, it was unfair to everyone around me. Letting someone else take my life was as if I were pulling the trigger myself. That thought sparked my "fail-safe."

Clearly, I survived. I survived by doing something that would only make sense in the movies. I put my car in reverse and drove straight into oncoming traffic. I reasoned that staying still or driving forward would lead to certain consequences. My best shot at survival was to take a reckless, dangerous risk. The gunman didn't follow. I guess it was too crazy—even for him.

Why share this with you?

The Hidden Costs

This near-death experience revealed a powerful truth about relationships: the way you relate to yourself and others can either be your greatest asset or your biggest vulnerability. When you cultivate healthy, self-aware relationships—both with yourself and others—they become a source of strength and support. But when those relationships are neglected or unbalanced, they can become a source of pain or destruction.

Just like any power, your ability to connect with others and yourself must be used with intention. Without it, the very thing that could lift you can instead pull you down, consuming your peace and well-being.

I hope you never get this close to experiencing firsthand the hidden costs of this extreme lesson. However if you:

1. Have experienced something similar,
2. Are currently experiencing burnout, sadness, or depression,
3. Are a survivor of emotional abuse or trauma,
4. Want to build relationships rooted in trust and happiness,

This book is for you. Its purpose is to guide you through navigating both personal and professional relationships in a way that empowers you to thrive, not just survive.

In this book, you will learn:

*   How to break free from past experiences that limit your ability to connect
*   A step-by-step method for building strong, meaningful, and authentic relationships
*   Strategies for maintaining healthy boundaries while deepening connections
*   How to identify, avoid, or break free from toxic relationships

Your Transformational Path

Your connections will be transformed when you recognize that empathy is your greatest superpower in relationships. It allows you to connect with others on a deep, trusting level and enables them to connect with you in return. But empathy can also become your greatest vulnerability.

When not properly balanced or protected, empathy can leave you open to emotional exhaustion, manipulation, or being overwhelmed by the emotions of others. Without healthy boundaries, this deep connection can become a burden. That's why it's essential to understand what healthy empathy is and how to navigate it with care and self-awareness.

Many people misunderstand what empathy truly is, and it's easy to see why. With so many conflicting definitions, confusion abounds. People often confuse empathy with sympathy. Sympathy involves recognizing another person's feelings without necessarily sharing or understanding them. Empathy, on the other hand, goes deeper—it requires both sharing and understanding their emotional experience.

Brené Brown, author of the book *Dare To Lead*, defines empathy as "connecting to the emotions that underpin (another person's) experience. It's the ability to relate to and feel what others feel."

Chris Voss, a former F.B.I. hostage negotiator and author of the book *Never Split the Difference*, defines empathy as "becoming utterly aware of the other person's perspective and understanding their viewpoint and emotions."

I like both of these definitions. Simplifying it further, I define empathy as the ability to feel what others feel and see things from their perspective. My own journey taught me that being selflessly empathetic without proper boundaries can lead to burnout, depression, and emotional exhaustion. I was giving endlessly, allowing others to drain my energy without reciprocation until I learned to transform my empathy into a source of strength.

Your Current Blueprint of Connection

We all come into adulthood with a blueprint for relationships. This blueprint isn't something we consciously create—it's formed through our earliest experiences, family dynamics, and significant relationships. My blueprint was shaped by witnessing my mother's sacrifice and resilience as a single parent, which instilled in me a deep capacity for empathy and an unconscious belief that love required putting others before myself at all costs.

Attachment Theory: The Science Behind Our Blueprints

This concept of relationship blueprints is rooted in psychological research. Pioneering studies by Dr. John Bowlby and Dr. Mary Ainsworth on attachment theory reveal that our early caregiving experiences create internal "working models" that influence how we navigate relationships throughout life. Their studies showed that these patterns—secure, anxious, avoidant, or disorganized—persist into adulthood and significantly influence our intimate relationships.

More recently, Dr. Amir Levine and Rachel Heller's research, highlighted in *Attached*, reveals how these early relationship templates become neurologically ingrained, creating automatic unconscious response patterns that influence our interactions and connections. Their studies reveal that people with different attachment styles perceive the same relationship events through completely different lenses shaping different perspectives.

Intergenerational Patterns: The Legacy We Inherit

The research on relationship patterns is equally compelling. Dr. Murray Bowen's family systems theory demonstrates how relationship dynamics are passed down and repeated across generations. Studies by Dr. Emily Greenfield show that children who witness unhealthy conflict resolution are significantly more likely to reproduce those same patterns in their own relationships, creating what she calls "emotional inheritance."

Research from The Gottman Institute found that children who grow up witnessing contempt and criticism between parents are more likely to struggle with emotional regulation and healthy conflict resolution in their relationships. Dr. John Gottman's longitudinal studies demonstrate that without intervention, these patterns tend to perpetuate across generations.

These early experiences become your relationship template— they determine how you approach connection, how you express love, and what you expect from others. We either mirror the behaviors modeled for us or attempt to compensate for past trauma and abuse. For some, these relationship templates mean adopting self-protection and emotional distance. For others, like myself, it manifests as overgiving and a lack of boundaries in empathy.

The Patterns We Repeat

When we don't understand our ingrained relationship templates, we're doomed to repeat them. I entered my marriage with unexamined expectations and patterns. I believed sacrificing my own needs and dreams was the price of love. I thought that being a good partner meant absorbing pain without complaint and that asking for support was a sign of weakness.

My wife, too, had her own unexamined templates. Neither of us understood how our past experiences were shaping our current relationship. We were unconsciously speaking different languages of connection, each perplexed by the other's inability to understand.

The Mirror of Relationships

Relationships serve as mirrors, reflecting to us our deepest beliefs about ourselves and others. When my wife couldn't offer the support I needed, it wasn't just about her response—it was about what that response triggered in me. It activated old wounds around abandonment and self-worth that I hadn't fully processed.

The way I felt at that moment—indifferent to whether I lived or died as a gun was pointed at me on Interstate 30—wasn't just about that single incident. It was the result of years of disconnection from myself. I had lost touch with my values, my voice, and my boundaries. In trying to be everything for everyone else, I had become nothing to myself. It became clear to me that without first understanding myself, true connection with others is impossible.

Self-Awareness: The Foundation of Connection

Self-awareness is the first and most essential step in building meaningful connections. You cannot authentically connect with others until you have connected with yourself. You cannot set healthy boundaries until you understand your needs and values. You cannot truly see others until you've seen yourself.

My journey back from that highway moment began with a radical commitment to self-understanding. I had to examine my relationship templates, identify my patterns, and reconnect with my worth. Only then could I begin to build genuinely nurturing relationships.

What about you? What relationship templates are you carrying? What patterns do you find yourself repeating? Understanding these is not self-indulgence—it's the critical foundation for everything that follows. Because once you understand yourself, you gain the power to choose differently. You transform from someone merely repeating unconscious patterns to someone who consciously creates the connections you desire.

Those of us blessed (or cursed) with high empathy often believe that our ability to feel others' pain makes us better at relationships. But empathy without boundaries isn't sustainable. It's like trying to fill others' cups while your own is empty.

Our journey begins with understanding the foundation of lasting impact: the P.A.C.T. you make for yourself and others.

KEY TAKEAWAYS

This chapter explored how past experiences shape our approach to connection and why understanding ourselves is a critical step in mastering meaningful relationships. Through my journey from deep connection to isolation and back, we have explored how:

- Our early experiences create relationship templates that influence how we connect with others
- The quality of our relationships profoundly impacts our health, wealth, and overall well-being
- Unexamined patterns from our past can lead us into destructive relationship dynamics
- Self-awareness serves as the foundation for authentic connection with others
- Empathy is a double-edged sword - both our greatest strength and potential vulnerability

As we move forward, remember that your journey to transformative relationships begins with turning inward. By understanding your relationship templates, you unlock the ability to break free from limiting patterns and cultivate thriving, authentic connections.

PART TWO

The P.A.C.T. Method: How Relationships Work

Communication is more than words—it's a complex dance of intention, understanding, and mutual respect. This section introduces the P.A.C.T. framework, breaking down the essential elements that transform ordinary interactions into meaningful connections. You'll learn how Purpose, Authenticity, Communication, and Trust intertwine to create relationships that are not only functional but truly transformative. These chapters will provide you with a new lens for understanding human interaction, uncovering the subtle yet powerful dynamics that allow some connections to flourish while others falter.

2

Understanding P.A.C.T.
in Relationships

What is the purpose of genuine connection in relationships? This question consumed me after a painful reunion with someone I once considered a close friend. For years, he lived overseas while I measured time by the moments I longed to share with him. When he finally returned to our hometown, I felt that familiar surge of excitement—finally, we could bridge the gap of those lost years together.

But something had shifted. The friend who once spent evenings on my couch discussing life's great mysteries now seemed to see me only through the lens of potential business value. Every call and every message carried the subtext of recruitment rather than reconnection. Our relationship, which had once been a sanctuary of authentic connection and mutual support, had transformed into something transactional—a business opportunity to be leveraged rather than a friendship to be cherished. As my unanswered texts piled up and our coffee meetings became sales pitches, I found myself mourning not just the friendship we once had, but questioning the very nature of human connection itself.

After a lifetime of repeated betrayal by people I thought I could trust the most, it seemed logical to avoid creating close relationships with people. By doing so, I would protect myself from hurt.

However, some of the greatest joys and accomplishments I've ever had in life were made possible by the relationships I had at the time. If I give up on relationships, I would also be giving up on the future best accomplishments and times of my life. I'm betting you can relate to this dilemma.

Defining a P.A.C.T. Relationship

A relationship, by its simplest definition, is two or more people who relate to each other; being linked or associated together through something shared in common. Connection in relationships is something we all want. Yet, there is no shortage of complaints lamenting how it's so hard to find people to connect to.

Research in social psychology underscores the importance of shared goals and values in forming deep connections. When individuals discover common ground, they are more likely to engage in meaningful interactions, fostering a sense of belonging and purpose. I call this forming a P.A.C.T.

Pact: An agreement or alliance between people.

Forming a P.A.C.T. is fundamental in nurturing the sense of belonging in every relationship. How? Belonging flourishes when there is **Purpose, Authenticity, Communication**, and **Trust**.

- **Purpose:** What motivates you most in life
- **Authenticity:** Your real values and character
- **Communication:** How you convey your true thoughts and feelings
- **Trust:** Reliable and dependable

These four foundational pillars create the acronym I call P.A.C.T., and a pact is exactly what you form in thriving relationships. My former client, Cara, helped me realize that bonding and building happy relationships through P.A.C.T. is not as elusive as it may seem.

Cara's Story

Cara is a former client of mine who would come to my group classes. Here's what you should know about Cara: She's all of five feet tall but has the presence of a six-foot-tall person. She is very smart, driven, and successful by societal standards. As an ER doctor, she regularly came to take my high-intensity workout classes as a way to both relieve stress and maintain good health. In every class, she outworked almost everyone in the room, man or woman. She always came to class with a smile and a great attitude, until one day she didn't.

On this particular day, she came to the workout studio later than usual. She did not smile or say hello as she typically would. Her face showed the tell-tale signs of exhaustion, sadness, and frustration. Being curious about the change in her demeanor, I walked over to her and asked, "Tough day?"

Until this point, Cara and I were acquaintances with a decent connection and relationship. What she said next seemed a little uncomfortable to say to someone you only know as an acquaintance. She decided to open up and be vulnerable with me.

"Today is a tough day," she said, looking down to avoid eye contact. "Work was very difficult. I feel sick and under the weather. I'm very disappointed that I'm not performing well in my workout. I feel like I should just quit this workout and go home."

This level of vulnerability is a big deal at this moment. We are talking about a very self-confident woman who strives to reach high standards in everything she does. She admitted out loud that she felt like a failure.

What would you say to Cara at this moment? Most people might say some version of "Don't beat yourself up" or "I believe in you. You can do it. Don't quit" or "You shouldn't feel this way..." Any version of these responses, however, makes a person feel unheard because it invalidates their current feelings.

So what can you say instead that would not invalidate their feelings, and be supportive? "Understandably, you feel this way because you usually lift stronger and run faster," I said. "An exceptionally tough day and feeling sick is a rare experience for you to endure a workout in." Validating her feelings, I added, "You may not have your best day every day, but you can do your best for today. Whatever that looks like today, I will be very proud of you for doing it, even if it's not up to your usual performance. I hope you are proud of it too." With that, a light smile formed, the first smile I had seen from her that day, and she went and finished her workout.

The crazy thing about connecting with people is that you don't always know the exact moment a deep connection and positive impact happens. This was the moment Cara and I grew our connection to something more meaningful, but I wouldn't know the full impact until a year later.

A year after that conversation with Cara, I got a promotion and my boss announced it to all the people I trained. I was a little surprised to receive a promotion after a little more than a year of coaching. I later found out that Cara was not surprised. One day after the announcement, Cara came to me and said, "Do you remember that day I had a bad day and was sick?"

"Yes," I replied.

"Do you remember what you said to me?" she asked.

"Yes," I said. "I remember that moment very clearly."

"Moments like that are why you deserve this promotion," she continued. She went on to explain how I was the first coach to remember her name and to genuinely get to know her, to care about her life outside her workout performance.

"I'm telling you this because you need to know that I'm not the only person who feels this way," Cara said. "All of us that come to this workout studio talk, and we all agree that you are the best coach because you authentically get to know us. So when I heard your boss and coworkers announce that you had gotten promoted, I was so happy for you."

Cara's words taught me something important: communication along with shared purpose, goals, and values causes connection and influence, and inspires people to give you more than the bare minimum effort. It's not about a title, tenure, status, money, or the amount of education and experience you have. It's about caring enough about others that you are genuinely curious to get to know them and help them fulfill their highest potential. It's about making them feel seen, heard, and validated in their best and worst moments. It's about creating and choosing a P.A.C.T. between you and others.

Remember, P.A.C.T is an acronym that stands for:

- Purpose
- Authenticity
- Communication
- Trust

When you and others share similar goals and values aligned with your **purpose, authenticity** comes naturally, and **trust** deepens over time. The only way to know if this kind of relationship can exist is through **communication.** That's what happened between Cara and me.

To illustrate further how communication helps build relationships that help you thrive, let me share with you an illustrative story about Sam and Alex. This story is based loosely on the actions of a few teachers that influenced me at a charter school I went to in my freshman and sophomore years..

Sam and Alex were colleagues at a charter school, working at the same grade level, but never really connecting on a personal level. That is until one day during a casual lunch conversation, they discovered a surprising shared passion that sparked a series of discussions, projects, and initiatives they spearheaded together, creating a bond that went beyond mere co-worker status.

Sam and Alex

In the bustling staff room, filled with chatter and laughter from teachers on their lunch break, Sam and Alex – two near-strangers – find themselves sharing a table amongst a sea of familiar faces. They exchange polite small talk about their classes and students, their unfamiliarity with each other is evident in the conversation. But as they converse, they discover a shared desire to make a difference at the school.

Sam expresses concern about the fleeting nature of the school year, lamenting the lack of memorable experiences. Alex, intrigued by this sentiment, proposes the idea of organizing a fundraiser to support a specific cause: renovating the school's outdated library to create a vibrant learning space. Sam and Alex envisioned the fundraiser as an opportunity not only to raise funds but also to foster a sense of unity within the school community.

Sam and Alex have met up several times to collaborate and their initial conversation at lunch is now a thriving project in the making. The hours spent in collaboration have only deepened their initial connection. Despite their initial unfamiliarity, they have worked closely together to develop a great strategy.

In a conference room, surrounded by meticulously crafted plans and colorful posters outlining the fundraiser's details, Sam commends Alex for his innovative ideas for fundraising activities, while Alex praises Sam's ability to mobilize support from the school staff and students. "Alex, your insights have shaped this project. I'm not sure it would have come this far without you," Sam commented. "And your organizational skills, Sam, have been the glue holding everything together. We make a great team," Alex replied.

As they worked, there was an undercurrent of mutual respect, a recognition of each other's strengths and contributions. Together, they marveled at how their collaboration had transformed a simple idea into a meaningful initiative that would benefit the entire school.

"You know, when we first sat down for lunch that day, I never imagined it would lead to this. I've come to trust your judgment and value our partnership," said Sam.

"Sam. With our combined efforts, who knows what else we can achieve!" replied Alex.

As they reviewed their plans, anticipation filled the room. Sam and Alex recognized that the fundraiser would not only enhance the school's learning environment but also strengthen the bonds within the community. Through their joint efforts, they forged a partnership founded on a shared commitment to making a positive impact.

This story exemplifies the essence of connection in relationships through the P.A.C.T Sam and Alex created. Relationship connections can be as brief as a lunch break, as long as a career, or even a lifetime. They can start with an introduction from mutual friends or by a chance meeting between strangers.

Connection is not about finding a replica of yourself but discovering shared values, interests, or goals that resonate on a deeper level. Connection can transform indifferent relationships into sources of inspiration and mutual support.

The story of Sam and Alex brings to light a critical aspect of human connection: it's often the shared purpose or values that bind us, rather than superficial similarities. Shared purpose was also what kept my former wife and I together for almost a decade, even through tough times. You might be surprised at how many people share similar values to you, regardless of age, gender, or race.

By understanding P.A.C.T., you can uncover and strengthen these connections, enhancing your sense of belonging and purpose and making building happy relationships easier. It will also help you understand why a relationship is not happy. With that understanding, you can make the appropriate improvement or end relationships that are not serving a mutually beneficial purpose.

KEY TAKEAWAYS

The stories of Sam, Alex, and Cara illustrate how relationships form through P.A.C.T. principles. In Sam and Alex's case, a casual lunch conversation evolved into a powerful partnership through shared purpose. Similarly, a simple "Tough day?" to Cara was the beginning of transforming a client relationship into a meaningful connection that impacted both lives.

Let's examine how both stories demonstrate each principle of P.A.C.T.:

Purpose
- Sam and Alex discovered their shared commitment to improving their school.
- Cara and I connected through our mutual dedication to personal growth and well-being.

Authenticity
- Sam and Alex recognized and appreciated each other's complementary strengths.
- Cara appreciated authentic care and attention, while I admired her dedication and resilience.

Communication
- Sam and Alex built trust through open dialogue and collaborative problem-solving.
- With Cara and I, genuine curiosity and validation created space for a deeper connection.

Trust
- Sam and Alex's partnership grew through consistent support and shared success.
- Cara's trust manifested in her willingness to be vulnerable and later advocate for my promotion.

These stories show us that forming a P.A.C.T. isn't about grand gestures or complex strategies. It's about authentic moments of connection—whether discovering shared values over lunch or showing genuine care during someone's tough day. When we align our purpose, demonstrate authentic attractiveness through character, communicate with genuine interest, and build trust through consistent actions, we create relationships that not only last but transform everyone within the pact.

As we move forward, we'll explore each element of P.A.C.T. in detail, providing you with the tools to create these meaningful connections in your own life. Every strong relationship begins with a moment of genuine connection—your next opportunity might be just a curious question away. Whether it is the barista making our coffee, a friend, or a future life partner. Just like Sam and Alex, and like Cara and myself, you might find unexpected common ground with someone you've only known superficially.

While these stories show how P.A.C.T. creates strong relationships, understanding the framework isn't enough. To truly master these principles, we must also understand what happens when they break down. In the next chapter, we'll discuss how the first principle of P.A.C.T, Purpose, can help your relationship succeed and how misalignment in purpose can cause devastating consequences.

Purpose:
Your Core Driver

Purpose drives everything we do, making it essential for those in your P.A.C.T. to support your purpose—and for you to support theirs. As a famous comedian once pointed out, one person can't say, "I'm going to church," while the other says, "I'm going to hit the (crack) pipe." Their values and goals are simply too different, making it nearly impossible to build a strong, lasting relationship.

However, people often confuse purpose with goals. Understanding this distinction is important for building lasting relationships.

Purpose vs Goals

Goals are externally driven and shaped by:

- Meeting work deadlines
- Achieving team goals
- Earning recognition
- Avoiding negative consequences

While these motivators can be powerful, they're often temporary. Once the reward is achieved or the threat passes, motivation fades.

Purpose, however, emerges from within shaped by:

- Core values
- Personal beliefs
- Deepest convictions
- Guiding principles

This internal drive for purpose, unlike a goal, never ends and creates lasting motivation and opportunities for deeper connections. When we connect with others through shared intrinsic purpose, relationships naturally flourish.

As we move forward, remember that every relationship principle shared has real-world implications. The stakes are high, but so are the rewards. By understanding what strengthens relationships—and what makes them fail—we can avoid heartbreak and build bonds that can thrive even through tough times.

The Real Stakes:
When Purpose Holds and When It Breaks

How does a nine-year marriage fail and end with a crash? The answer reveals both the strength and vulnerability of our deepest relationships. My first marriage is proof that these principles aren't just theories. They are vital truths that can either support or ruin our most important relationships.

I met a woman whose intelligence and dedication to helping others perfectly aligned with my mission in life. We both had a deep desire to make a difference and support those in need. At the time, our way of doing so was through the congregation of the church we regularly attended. My then-wife excelled at offering practical support– she was quick to provide means for those who were sick, emotionally struggling, or facing financial hardship. I, on the other hand, thrived on building relationships, creating a space where people felt safe sharing their deepest struggles and joys. Our complementary strengths and shared sense of purpose became the foundation of our relationship—strong enough to weather what could have been a devastating early storm.

During our honeymoon in 2007, I lost my job. The Great Recession was beginning, and jobs were scarce. Depression hit me hard—the kind that makes you question your worth as a partner, as a provider, as a man. But our relationship not only survived; it thrived. My wife stood by me, never making me feel lesser, embodying the very spirit of service that had drawn us together.

This tension might have broken lesser relationships, but our shared purpose—helping others—kept us together. It would be two long years before I found steady work again. Until then, I worked odd jobs in unskilled manual labor for a sprinkler company and a landscape company. I also got my insurance license but failed to be productive in selling insurance at that time. In one of those two years, we made a combined $25,000 after taxes. This amount of income was too much for subsidized health care at the time, but it was too little for us to afford health insurance on our own. I do not know how we survived! Yet, through all that tension and stress, we were still more effective as a team than as individuals in pursuing and fulfilling our shared purpose. This truth sustained us for nearly a decade.

But as the years passed, something began to shift. I began to grow and change, pursuing personal development and new interests and our purposes began to diverge. But what I saw as a positive change, my wife experienced as something entirely different. To her, it felt like I was drifting away from the mission we had built together — and in many ways, from her. Despite nearly a decade together, this misalignment of purpose eventually led to the breakdown of trust and communication. I wanted to keep growing and finding new ways to serve the world. She, however, clung to the life and mission we had built together. Conversations that once felt like *partnership* began to feel like *opposition*. Trust and communication began to quietly erode, even as we still shared a home.

The final conversation that ended our nine-year marriage centered on this loss of shared purpose. When I suggested we could work through our issues together, my wife's response was telling: "No. These friends are my family now." indicating that she had given up on our family and adopted a new group of friends as her family. Our once strong connection, based on shared goals and values, faded. Now, individual survival mattered more than our shared vision.

In that moment, nine years of shared purpose, trust, and dreams crumbled to dust. We had simply grown in different directions, and neither of us knew how to bridge the gap.

The Lessons Learned

This experience taught me an important lesson: While shared purpose can keep a relationship strong during tough times, without it, even the strongest bonds can break.

Mutual support of purpose in relationships is not just "nice to have"—it is essential for relationships to survive and thrive. When relationships work, they can support us through our darkest moments. When they fail, they can create those dark moments.

Purpose in Action: Sam and Alex's Story

Remember Sam and Alex from our last chapter? A casual lunch conversation took a turn when Sam and Alex discovered their shared commitment to improving the school. This wasn't just about raising money to renovate a library - it reflected their core values about doing what's best for kids' education.

Their partnership flourished because:

- They connected through shared values, not just shared tasks
- Their individual strengths served a common purpose
- Their motivation came from internal conviction, not external pressure

Over time, their environmental initiatives expanded beyond the workplace. They organized community clean-ups, advocated for sustainable practices, and inspired others to join their cause. Their relationship deepened through this shared mission.

The Challenge of Defining Purpose in a Pressured World

Society often presents a narrow, prescribed path to success: get a good job, get married, and start a family. Friends and family frequently reinforce these expectations with well-intentioned but limiting questions. "Why are you still single?" "When are you going to settle down?" "What are you going to do with your life?" "When will you give me a grandbaby?" These questions reveal a fundamental misunderstanding of purpose.

True purpose isn't fulfilling a checklist of what others expect. It's not about reaching societal milestones or giving in to family pressures. Instead, it is a deeply personal flame that burns from within—something that energizes and challenges you, giving meaning to your daily existence.

Many people mistake goals for purpose. They chase achievements that look good on paper but fail to ignite their inner passion. A college degree, a prestigious job, or a traditional relationship might seem like success to others, but if these don't resonate with your core being, they become hollow pursuits. When we follow external paths, it can create shallow relationships. Instead of connecting through real passion, you may find yourself always looking for validation from others.

Your purpose is something that makes you eager to wake up each morning. It's a calling to pursue even if no one notices; even if it means struggling with a smile. When you're aligned with your true purpose, you attract more of the kind of people who transform your relationships. Instead of seeking partners or connections that simply support your goals and measure up to societal expectations and norms, you'll attract and cultivate relationships that understand and celebrate your deepest self.

The danger of misaligned purpose is profound. Relationships built on external expectations rather than internal passion become fragile. You'll find yourself drifting apart, wondering why the initial connection has faded. By contrast, when you share a strong connection with others and deeply respect each other's authentic purposes, relationships become rich, supportive, and transformative.

Finding Purpose:
The Path to Authentic Relationships

How can you find your purpose and create these connections? You can do this in three simple steps. **The first step is to know and understand your purpose.** Here are some tips to get you started on accomplishing step one:

Ask yourself:

- What matters most deeply to you?
- Which activities energize rather than drain you?
- What would you do even if no one noticed?

- Where do you naturally want to make a difference?
- What experiences in life made you feel the most joy, excitement, and happiness?

Your answers uncover your deep-rooted purpose—the key to authentic connections. These questions have even greater impact when a friend asks them, especially the last one. A friend can help identify common threads in your experiences of joy, bringing greater clarity to your purpose and how to articulate it.

The second step is to communicate your purpose clearly and succinctly. The book, *Start With Why*, and its sequel, *Find Your Why*, both by Simon Sinek, give great detail on how to find, understand, and articulate your purpose.

A simple, clear way to articulate your purpose is by completing this sentence.

My purpose it to help people _____ so that_____

For me, I've discovered that my purpose is to help people be the best versions of themselves so that we can better thrive in the communities we live in. By doing steps one and two, you will attract others that align with you.

The third step is to pursue actions and connections that align with your purpose. This third step will put you in more environments where you are likely to find more people that align with you. To act on my purpose, I choose careers that promoted teamwork in communities and groups focused on self-improvement. My career in fitness aligns with this purpose. Coaching people on leadership, relationship, and communication skills also align with this purpose. It's a privilege to understand why I love what I do, and to be able to intentionally move into things I love with people I love doing it with. I connect with people who commit to self-improvement. This helps us build authentic relationships. As you move toward your purpose, you'll meet others on a similar path that support your purpose.

Now it begs the question, what if your purpose does not align, or is not complimentary to another's? Does that mean there is no relationship to be had? Not necessarily. Relationships exist on relationship levels, and not all relationships require deep connections. However, that does not mean there can not be a functional relationship at some level.

To illustrate, consider the relationship between cows and the cattle egret. If you've ever driven by a field full of cows, you may have noticed white birds all over the field. Those birds are called Cattle Egrets. What could a bird and a cow possibly share in common? The answer: not much. They do not share a purpose in life that's mutually complementary. Why do they coexist? As cows move through the field, they stir up insects. These unearthed insects become an easy source of food for these birds. This relationship only benefits the Egrets while having no negative effects, risks, or inconveniences to the cows. They have a functional relationship.

Similarly, orchids grow on a tree. The orchid benefits from the tree's height while the tree remains unaffected. It is possible to have a purely functional relationship. Right now you may be thinking of some people at work or school that fit this description. These kinds of relationships can be appreciated and are oftentimes beautiful in their own way. These relationships are still authentic, just not as deep as your closest relationships will be, and that's ok. These relationships help the world function.

We now understand that there are purpose-centered relationships and functional relationships, but you might be thinking, "What if the relationship is not neutral or functional, but rather toxic?" When you understand your purpose, you will be able to more quickly identify which relationships threaten to sabotage it and avoid toxic connections. This knowledge and understanding will help you make quick decisions on whether a relationship is emotionally safe or toxic for you.

The path to understanding your purpose and the relationships that align and support your purpose requires courage. It means listening to your inner voice over external expectations. It means being willing to explore what truly lights you up, even if it looks different from what others envision for you. It also means being willing to weather the storms that threaten to destroy even the strongest purposeful relationships, using shared purpose to keep these relationships going strong.

Knowing your purpose helps you see which relationships to keep and which to release. However, even strong connections will face challenges. Seafaring traditions offer a powerful metaphor for resilience. Let's explore this idea further.

Tie Yourself To The Boat

One of the ways we can learn how to navigate difficult times in life and keep our relationships strong is by looking at experienced sailors in history. Life and relationships will encounter storms, but shared purpose can be the thing that anchors you when you encounter them. Sometimes sailors would find themselves in a storm they could not sail themselves out of. In such circumstances, the only priority was to survive, but how? They would drop anchor, tie themselves to the boat, and wait for the storm to pass.

Similarly, when life gets rough, how can you weather the storm? Sometimes the best way is to prioritize your purpose. Anchor down and tie yourself to your boat, or purpose. This will help you simplify your focus until the storm passes. This works in both personal and professional relationships.

For example, in personal relationships, life storms by way of disagreements, financial struggles, or a health crisis will likely arise.

When they do, you can anchor down by taking care of the priorities. Make sure you and your family are housed and fed. Then tie yourself to the purpose that you and your significant other share. This shared and simplified focus during the stormy times in life will help you get through it together, and come out of it better "sailors" or life partners more capable of supporting each other than ever before.

Professional relationships, disagreements, organizational changes, and financial stress in the economy are going to happen from time to time. In these moments it's crucial to anchor down to the fundamentals of what the business needs to survive. It's also very important that you and those you work with tie yourself to the unified purpose of why you and your team work together beyond the reason for a paycheck. After the storm passes a sense of loyalty with you and your team will grow and become very hard to break.

Building Purpose-Driven Relationships

During challenging times, the strength of your relationships can make all the difference. Beyond shared interests or circumstances, the true foundation of lasting connections is a deeper sense of purpose. When relationships are built on mutual respect, shared values, and a commitment to growth, they become more resilient and fulfilling. Below are key insights into building purpose-driven relationships that stand the test of time.

1. You don't need identical purposes to connect.
True connection doesn't need identical ambitions. It thrives on mutual respect for each other's unique paths. The best relationships often grow between people with different purposes. These differences weave a rich tapestry of strengths and views. When you respect someone else's authentic purpose and they respect yours, you create space for individual growth and deep connection.

2. Complementary purposes often create the strongest, most enduring bonds.

Like puzzle pieces that fit perfectly together, relationships thrive when each person's purpose fills gaps or enhances the capabilities of the other. These complementary dynamics—where one person's visionary thinking balances another's practical execution, or one's nurturing nature complements another's protective instincts—create partnerships greater than the sum of their parts. The synergy that emerges from well-matched but different purposes generates both remarkable outcomes and deeply fulfilling and lasting connections. This balance allows each person to contribute their strengths while relying on the other in areas where they may lack, creating mutual growth and trust.

3. Shared values matter more than shared activities.

The foundation of lasting relationships isn't built on enjoying the same hobbies but on honoring the same core principles about how to live and treat others. Two people may pursue wildly different passions yet maintain an unbreakable bond through shared commitments to integrity, compassion, growth, or service. These common values create a shared language that transcends surface-level compatibility and allows for authentic understanding even when life paths diverge.

4. Purpose alignment naturally strengthens over time.

Like trees whose roots gradually intertwine beneath the soil, purpose-driven relationships deepen with each shared challenge and celebration. The recognition of shared purpose deepens into an intuitive understanding as you support each other's growth and stay committed through life's changes and challenges. This organic strengthening creates relationships that become more resilient and meaningful over time, making investing in purpose-aligned connections one of life's most valuable long-term assets.

Reflection Exercise

- Identify three activities that deeply energize you.
- List your core values driving these activities.
- Note relationships where these values align.
- Invest more time with people who are more purpose-aligned connections.

The power of purpose in forming deep, meaningful connections cannot be overstated. By understanding and embracing purpose, we can cultivate relationships that are not only fulfilling but also impactful. We also create relationships that not only last but transform both parties. It's the shared values and principles that not only bring us together but also keep us connected through thick and thin.

In a romantic relationship, this would mean that instead of focusing primarily on the goal of getting married and/or having kids (both are goals because as soon as the wedding or kids are had, the goal has been completed) you will instead focus first on understanding what drives you and your life partner to thrive in life, and then support that deeper purpose. That is a fulfilling purpose-driven relationship!

In a professional relationship, it's not about just doing the job, checking the boxes, and collecting the paycheck. Like that of Sam and Alex, we can instead turn casual connections into meaningful partnerships that serve something greater than ourselves.

─────────── *KEY TAKEAWAYS* ───────────

Purpose that is mutually supported serves as the invisible thread that binds us together in relationships and helps us survive through life's challenges. We've explored how purpose differs fundamentally from goals—while goals are temporary destinations often driven by external expectations, purpose is an internal compass that guides our entire journey. My painful divorce taught me that even strong relationships can break when shared purpose falls out of sync. In contrast, Sam and Alex's story highlights how shared goals can turn casual friends into strong allies.

We've learned that discovering your authentic purpose requires looking inward, beyond societal expectations and prescribed milestones. Through practical exercises and reflection, you've begun to identify what truly energizes you and gives your life meaning. We've also seen that not all relationships need to be deeply purpose-aligned to be valuable—some, like the cattle egret and cow, can be functionally beneficial without deep connection. Most importantly, we've discovered that purpose-driven relationships don't require identical passions but rather complementary strengths united by shared values, creating bonds that naturally strengthen over time.

Now it's your turn to transform understanding into action. This week, commit to three purposeful steps that will revolutionize your relationships:

First, schedule reflection time to complete the purpose exercise in this chapter. Don't rush this process—the clarity you gain will become your relationship compass for years to come. Write down your purpose statement and place it somewhere you'll see it daily.

Second, identify one relationship in your life that feels misaligned or draining. Have the courage to evaluate whether this connection supports your purpose or undermines it. If it's the latter, determine one specific boundary you can establish to protect your purpose.

Finally, reach out to someone whose purpose seems complementary to yours—someone you admire but haven't connected deeply with. Invite them for coffee or a meaningful conversation specifically about what drives you both. Come prepared to articulate your purpose clearly and listen deeply to theirs.

Remember, every transformative relationship begins with this fundamental truth: when you honor your authentic purpose and connect with others who respect that journey, you create not just relationships, but relationships that matter. The storms will come—they always do—but with purpose as your anchor, you'll weather them together, emerging stronger on the other side.

In the next chapter, we'll explore how Authenticity - the second element of P.A.C.T. - builds on this purposeful foundation.

4

Authenticity:
Beyond the Surface

R esearch suggests that the better you take care of your appearance, the more attractive you are initially. However, have you ever met someone you found attractive at first, but then said or did something that immediately made them less attractive? The magnetic pull between people extends far beyond physical attraction. In our daily interactions, we're drawn to certain individuals not just because of their appearance, but because of something deeper - their character, competence, and authentic way of being.

Understanding True Authenticity

Authenticity is the second pillar in P.A.C.T. in which the "A" stands for "Authenticity." When we talk about what we find authentic and attractive in relationships, we're not focusing on superficial physical qualities, but discussing deeper qualities that create lasting connection and respect.

Think about someone you deeply admire. Chances are, what attracts you to them goes far beyond the surface. Here are some qualities you might admire in this person:

☑ Their unwavering integrity in difficult situations

Integrity supports trust. When someone consistently demonstrates alignment between their words and actions, we're drawn to their commitment to integrity. We know a person who stays principled under pressure will be reliable. This reliability gives us emotional and mental safety and lets us be vulnerable without fear of betrayal. This deepens our connection in ways that charm and appearance alone cannot.

☑ The natural confidence they bring to challenges

Authentic confidence—not to be confused with arrogance—attracts others because it signals internal security. When someone approaches difficulties with calm assurance rather than desperate validation-seeking, they create an emotional safe space for others.. This genuine self-belief is contagious; it makes us believe that challenges can be overcome. We're naturally drawn to people who make us feel more capable, and who help us access our courage rather than feeding our insecurities.

☑ Their genuine interest in others' success

Few qualities attract us more powerfully than feeling truly seen and supported. When someone celebrates our wins without jealousy and helps us through setbacks without judgment, we experience the rare gift of being valued for who we are, not just what we provide. This authentic interest in others' growth creates relationship abundance rather than scarcity. People naturally gravitate toward those who make them feel significant rather than small, creating connections that build others up instead of creating competition.

☑ The competence they demonstrate

Competence draws us in displaying substance over showmanship. When someone truly masters a skill but stays humble, we admire their talent and modesty. They let their results shine instead of their ego. This balanced self-awareness creates space for others to contribute rather than compete. We're attracted to people whose competence makes the entire group better rather than those who use skills to dominate or diminish others.

☑ **Their dedication to personal growth and learning**

A growth mindset fosters relationships that evolve rather than stagnate. When someone views life as a journey of growth, they bring energy and possibility to every interaction. This mindset is attractive because it leads to a relationship that expands instead of restricts. It welcomes change rather than fights it. We are drawn to people who inspire us to grow by showing the value of ongoing self-improvement.

These qualities act like magnets, drawing people together in ways that superficial attributes never could. They create connections built on respect rather than utility, admiration rather than obligation, and growth rather than self-gratification. When authenticity becomes the foundation of our relationships, we create bonds that don't just endure challenges—they thrive through them.

The Balance of Inner and Outer Authenticity

In today's image-focused society, we often overemphasize external appearance while undervaluing inner qualities. Social media platforms and dating apps have amplified this imbalance, reducing complex human beings to carefully curated snapshots and surface-level impressions.

Physical appearance undeniably plays a role in initial attraction—it's our evolutionary programming at work. However, this first impression is merely an entry point, not the foundation for meaningful connection. Think of physical attraction as the door that might open initially, but authentic character is the room we actually want to spend time in.

While physical attraction might spark initial interest, it's the authenticity of character that resonates with and deepens connections over time. Long-term relationship satisfaction relies more on authenticity, emotional responsiveness, and shared values than on physical attraction. The most fulfilling relationships strike a balance: they acknowledge the reality of physical attraction while prioritizing the deeper qualities that create lasting bonds. This balance reflects true authenticity—honoring both our human nature and our higher capacities for connection.

Authenticity in Action:
Elena and Marcus's Professional Partnership

I met a woman named Elena when I was coaching a group fitness class. She would take my class regularly for about a year. She was a retired project manager from an energy company. One day outside of the gym we started to talk about experiences in inspiring and leading groups of people. She told me a story about when, before she retired, she met a man named Marcus during a conference. I'll reiterate the story to the best of my memory because it highlights how powerful authenticity can be to influence and attract people.

As Elena describes Marcus at first glance he didn't fit the typical image of a charismatic leader. He wasn't the most polished speaker, and his presentation slides were far from slick. But something about him captured the entire room's attention.

As Marcus shared his research on renewable energy solutions, Elena noticed something extraordinary. His passion wasn't about self-promotion or impressive credentials. Instead, he spoke with genuine humility about the communities he'd worked with, highlighting the innovative solutions local residents had developed.

During the Q&A session, a young researcher challenged one of Marcus's key findings. What could have been a defensive moment became a masterclass in authentic attractiveness. Marcus listened intently, his body language open and curious. "That's an excellent point," he responded. "Your observation helps me see a blind spot in our current research. Would you be interested in collaborating to explore that perspective further?"

The room was collectively impressed. Here was a seasoned researcher not just accepting criticism, but seeing it as an opportunity for growth and collaboration.

After the conference, Elena approached Marcus. "I've never seen someone handle a challenging question with such grace," she said. Marcus smiled, deflecting the praise. "It's not about me. It's about our shared goal of finding better solutions."

Their conversation revealed Marcus's true attractive authenticity. It wasn't about his appearance or even his impressive credentials. It was about:

- His unwavering integrity in handling difficult conversations
- The natural confidence he brought to intellectual challenges
- His genuine interest in others' success
- The humble competence he demonstrated without a hint of arrogance
- His dedication to personal and collective growth

Over the next few months, Elena and Marcus collaborated on a groundbreaking project. Their partnership flourished not because of external achievements, but because of their mutual respect and complementary strengths. Marcus's ability to listen, learn, and lift others up combined with Elena's execution and delegation created a collaborative environment where innovation thrived.

When their project received a major industry award, Marcus insisted on sharing the stage with his entire team, including Elena. "This success belongs to all of us," he said. "Each person here brought something unique and valuable."

At that moment, Elena understood how true authenticity influences others and attracts people to you and your cause. It isn't about trying to be the most impressive person in the room. It is about creating an environment where everyone feels valued, heard, and capable of contributing their best. It's about modeling behavior where people can be themselves and be celebrated and encouraged to do so.

This partnership demonstrated how authentic character traits like integrity, empathy, and competence attract the right people for sustainable, growing relationships. Marcus' magnetic quality came not from trying to impress but from his genuine interest in seeing what makes other people impressive and nurturing the potential in others.

The Courage to Be Unapologetically You

In our quest for connection and acceptance, we often fall into a common trap: presenting a carefully curated version of ourselves to the world. We might downplay our enthusiasm for niche interests, soften our opinions, or hide parts of our personality that we fear might be judged. This "watering down" of our authentic selves creates a paradox – in trying to become more appealing to everyone, we become less compelling to anyone.

The Trap of Self-Dilution

Consider what happens when you dilute a vibrant color. What was once striking becomes muted and forgettable. The same principle applies to our authentic selves. When we blend away our distinctive edges, we lose the very qualities that make us memorable and meaningful to others.

This self-dilution takes many forms:

- The executive who hides her passion for fantasy novels to appear more "serious"
- The new team member who nods along with the group consensus despite having valuable alternative perspectives

- The friend who downplays his accomplishments to avoid standing out
- The partner who suppresses emotional needs to maintain peace and harmony

Each instance represents a missed opportunity – not just for self-expression, but for genuine connection. The truth is, we don't connect deeply with watered-down versions of people; we connect with their unfiltered humanity.

The Hidden Cost of Pretense

When we consistently present a curated self to the world, we pay a significant psychological price. Research in social psychology shows that "impression management" – the constant monitoring and adjustment of our self-presentation – consumes valuable cognitive resources. This vigilance creates a state of persistent low-grade stress, as we're perpetually on guard against revealing our true selves.

More profoundly, this pretense cuts us off from the very connections we seek. Authentic relationships require vulnerability and transparency. When we hide behind carefully constructed facades, we create relationships with those facades, not with our true selves. The result is a peculiar form of loneliness – being surrounded by people who know our performance but not our person.

The Magnetic Power of Authenticity

Paradoxically, the qualities we often try to hide are frequently the very elements that draw others to us most powerfully:

- Your quirky humor creates memorable moments of joy.
- Your passionate enthusiasm for obscure topics reveals your capacity for depth.

- Your willingness to respectfully disagree demonstrates intellectual integrity.
- Your openness about your struggles fosters connection through shared humanity.

As author and researcher Brené Brown highlights in her work on vulnerability, what we often see as "flaws" can become powerful bridges to connection. It's in the parts of ourselves that feel most tender and exposed that our most authentic human bonds are formed.

Finding the Courage to Be Unapologetically You

Embracing your authentic self isn't about abandoning all social awareness or imposing your personality on every situation. Rather, it's about discerning when adaptability serves growth versus when it betrays your core self. The following are practices that support genuine authenticity:

1. Practice self-awareness without self-judgment. Regularly reflect on which aspects of your self-presentation feel aligned versus performative. Notice without criticism when you've tempered your true reactions.

2. Start with trusted spaces. Begin expressing your unfiltered self with those who have demonstrated they value authenticity. These environments provide safe practice grounds.

3. Embrace the discomfort of being seen. Recognize that the vulnerability of showing your true self comes with temporary discomfort that yields to deeper connection.

4. Seek environments that celebrate your authentic self. Rather than changing yourself to fit environments, gravitate toward people and places that appreciate your genuine nature.

5. Authenticity attracts authenticity. When you lead by example, showing up as your true self, you encourage others to do the same—creating a ripple effect of genuine connection.

The Paradox of Authentic Appeal

The irony is that striving to please everyone often makes us less appealing, while embracing our true selves may attract fewer people—but those connections will be far deeper and more meaningful. Not everyone will resonate with your authentic self—and that's not just okay, it's necessary. Genuine connection isn't built on universal appeal but on authenticity and alignment with the right people.

As author and entrepreneur Seth Godin notes, "If you try to appeal to everyone, you'll appeal to no one." Those who are drawn to your authentic self will form deeper, more meaningful connections than a hundred surface-level admirers ever could.

Think of authenticity as a filter, not a performance. It won't make you universally popular, but it will attract the right people—those who connect with the real you. And those are the connections that truly matter.

In a world of careful curation and strategic self-presentation, having the courage to be unapologetically you isn't just refreshing – it's revolutionary. It creates space for others to do the same, fostering environments where people can thrive as their full, complex, and gloriously imperfect selves.

The Ripple Effect of Authenticity

When you commit to authentic living, you create a ripple effect that extends far beyond your immediate relationships. You give others permission to be authentic, creating spaces where genuine connection can flourish.

In professional settings, your authenticity transforms transactional relationships into meaningful collaborations. In personal relationships, it creates the safety needed for deep intimacy.

In community settings, it builds trust that enables collective action.

Most importantly, authentic living means matching your actions with your values. This creates integrity and coherence, which feels deeply satisfying. The path to authenticity can be tough. It often involves confronting uncomfortable truths about ourselves. However, the rewards of living and connecting from this place are immeasurable.

KEY TAKEAWAYS

The role of Authenticity emerges as a component that helps deepen our connections, especially in starting and sustaining relationships. Within a P.A.C.T., we understand that true attraction in relationships extends far beyond the physical. It also includes admiration for someone's skills, personality, and character that truly draws us closer and enriches our connections.

Physical appearance plays a role in initial attraction, but authentic character creates lasting bonds. By practicing integrity, cultivating genuine confidence, developing real interest in others, and balancing internal and external authenticity, you can develop an authentic attractiveness that draws the right people to you.

Authenticity isn't about perfection—it's about aligning your inner values with your outward actions. When we embrace this deeper understanding of Authenticity, the second pillar of P.A.C.T., we create space for more meaningful relationships, both personally and professionally, and find greater fulfillment in our work. Look beyond the surface and appreciate the deeper qualities that make our connections truly authentic.

Communication:
The Bridge to Connection

Communication isn't just one element of a relationship - it's the essential link that makes all other elements possible. Just as a bridge connects two separate lands, communication bridges the gap between individual perspectives, creating pathways for understanding and connection.

Think about the last time you felt truly understood. Chances are, it wasn't just about the words communicated, but how they were received. Effective communication creates an understanding where all parties feel seen, heard, and valued.

The Universal Challenge

Whether you are a survivor of emotional abuse and trauma, or not, we all face a universal challenge. Think about this: A musician might feel completely at home on stage but terrified to give a public speech. A CEO could command a boardroom yet feel lost on a first date. A brilliant scientist might understand the cosmos but struggle to connect at a social gathering. Our confidence and our ability to connect with others shifts dramatically depending on the situation.

But there's one skill that transcends all these scenarios—one ability that affects every interaction, every relationship, every moment of human connection. This skill is the third pillar, the "C", in P.A.C.T. called "Communication." You always have everything you need to use this skill effectively. The challenge isn't acquiring new tools—it's learning to use what you already have more effectively.

Mastering communication might be one of the hardest and most rewarding challenges you'll ever undertake. It demands both technical skill and emotional intelligence, requiring us to be both strategic and authentic, planned and spontaneous, confident and vulnerable.

The 3 Keys of
Effective, Empathetic Communication

I've trained for over a decade in a School for Public Speaking through the church I grew up in. That school taught me how to connect with an audience through presentation and preparedness. I spent another decade inspiring groups of adults to do hard things and coached staff members to perform to their potential.

I've learned the following 3 communication principles through practice, study, and more practice, and we are going to unpack these in this chapter:

1. Empathy + Communication is the key to lasting connection in happy relationships.
2. Traditional communication training fails you, especially naturally empathetic people.
3. The quality of your relationships dictate the quality of your career, marriage, and life.

Empathic communication is powerful in making connections with people. This isn't just theory - it's the result of over 20 years practicing the art and science of communication, and I love everything about it!

With these principles in mind, it's important to know how to create connections with the right people, how to protect yourself from the connections that harm you, and how to navigate working with difficult people when there's no other option. This is important because the very empathy that can unsuspectingly invite toxic environments is also the key to our greatest influence. The question isn't whether you're too empathetic in your communication - it's whether you're wielding that empathy effectively. Harnessing your naturally empathetic senses, along with highly effective communication skills is the way.

Why Traditional Communication Training Fails

This brings us to why traditional communication training often fails people like us. Can you remember the last corporate training you went to that talked about "soft" skills? There was probably a section of that training that talked about conflict resolution, how to have difficult conversations, or how to make people feel seen and heard. They probably said "Active listening is the key!" but didn't clearly explain what that is.

Do you remember trying those suggestions, and them not working as well as the corporate trainers said they would?

In my experience, many corporate training sessions offer advice that sounds appealing but lacks clarity and real-world effectiveness. What's worse is when leaders do not model the behaviors taught in these sessions. When that happens, the push for better communication can feel fake and manipulative, especially to empathetic individuals. When you and others in the company attempt to apply the training advice, it can unintentionally come off as insincere because the focus shifts to ticking boxes of the "right way" to communicate instead of fostering genuine connections.

Here's the truth—the simple formula for influence and connection is as follows:

Empathy + Communication = Connection

Traditional training fails because it treats empathy as a soft skill to manage. But empathy isn't just a skill - it's a power source. When channeled correctly, it becomes the foundation of authentic and thriving connection.

Empathetic communication is crucial to creating the best and happiest relationships in your professional and personal life. Displaying and communicating empathy in a way that is both safe for you and felt by others is the hardest part of connecting with others. This book intends to codify the process into a simple method that you can apply to anyone at any time of your choosing. When you do, not only will you attract healthier relationships, but you will also see advancement in your careers and your overall well-being.

When I look back on my history, I can easily identify the polarizing consequences and benefits that manifested when I violated or adhered to the timeless principles of communication and relationships. This section on communication will show you how to apply timeless principles so you can thrive in your relationships and live your best life.

Sam and Alex: Communication in Action

Let's refer back to Sam and Alex's collaboration mentioned in chapters 2 and 3. Can you imagine their success being possible without good communication with each other? Hardly. The same can be said for Marcus's ability, discussed in Chapter 4, to successfully bring a team together that led to a prestigious award.

It becomes clear that their success wasn't solely based on shared purpose or mutual attractiveness. Effective communication was a must to sustain their partnership and overall success.

For Sam and Alex, their relationship started with a simple conversation in which they resonated over something meaningful. Remember how their communication evolved:

- Initial small talk turned into a shared vision
- Different viewpoints became complementary perspectives
- Challenges became opportunities for deeper understanding
- Feedback strengthened rather than strained their communication and connection

During one crucial project meeting, they faced a significant budget setback. Instead of letting frustration derail their progress, their communication skills shone through:

"I'm concerned about these numbers," Sam began carefully. "What are your thoughts on this?"

Alex paused, pondering the question. "I share your concern. Let's break this down together and see what options we may have missed."

This exchange exemplifies three critical elements:

1. Open expression of concerns
2. Invitation for perspective
3. Collaborative problem-solving

Despite different personalities and approaches, they found a way to share ideas, express concerns, and provide feedback in a manner that was constructive and respectful. They mutually felt seen and heard. This open line of communication allowed them to navigate challenges, celebrate successes, and continually align their efforts toward their shared environmental goals.

The Oxygen of Relationships

Quality communication acts like oxygen in relationships:

- It gives life to new connections
- Sustains existing bonds
- Allows growth and adaptation
- Enables healing when needed

Beyond words, effective communication involves:

- Empathy
- Emotional awareness
- Appropriate timing
- Tactfulness
- Mutual respect

Communication is the pipeline through which all other elements of a relationship flow. Without it, no relationship exists. It enables the sharing of information, the clarification of intentions, and the expression of emotions. Without quality communication, relationships stagnate and misunderstandings flourish.

Communication is not just about speaking but also about listening, understanding, and responding appropriately. We will elaborate on this more in Part 3 of this book regarding Toxic vs. Attractive Communication. Until then, below are a few questions I've seen great communicators reflect on that you can also begin to think about for yourself.

On a scale of 1 to 10, 10 being the best:

1. How well do you listen without planning your response?
2. Can you express concerns without triggering defensiveness?

3. Can you listen to feedback without being quick to be triggered into defensiveness?

4. Do you check for understanding in important conversations?

5. How often do you invite others' perspectives?

You, too, can reflect on your communication style and its impact on your relationships. If you rate yourself as a 9 or 10 on the questions above, that's great! If you see room for improvement, Part Three of this book will help you refine your skills through the 3 C's of Attractive Communication—curiosity, clarity, and courtesy.

Through the lens of P.A.C.T., communication is the lifeline that sustains and enriches relationships. By applying the 3 C's, you can foster meaningful connections, strengthen trust, and enhance trust and collaboration.

——————— KEY TAKEAWAYS ———————

When it comes to building deep, meaningful relationships, communication is everything. It's the invisible thread that holds every other element of connection together. Without it, even the strongest relationships can unravel. But when you combine Empathy + Communication — what I call Attractive Communication — something powerful happens. Your relationships become stronger, more fulfilling, and more connected than you ever thought possible.

Here's the good news: Attractive Communication isn't some elusive gift reserved for a select few — it's a skill you can learn and master. And once you do, you'll notice a shift in the way people respond to you, connect with you and even fight for you. If you want to build relationships that not only survive but thrive, quality communication is an absolute must.

- Belief in mutual good intentions
- Faith in shared commitment

When these elements align, relationships develop a resilience that can weather any storm. Let's take a look at how trust played an important factor in Diego and Sophia's relationship.

Trust in Action:
Sophia and Diego's Relationship Evolution

Within the warm, sunlit kitchen of their small apartment, Sophia and Diego found themselves in a rare moment of deep reflection. Their relationship, now entering its fifth year, had weathered challenges that would have torn apart less resilient partnerships.

Their trust developed through distinct stages of vulnerability and support:

Initial Testing

Diego remembered their early days when Sophia had shared her struggles with anxiety—something she had hidden from previous partners. "I was terrified you'd see me as broken," she had confided. Instead of recoiling, Diego had listened with compassion, asking how he could support her.

Growing Through Challenges

Their first real test came when Diego lost his job unexpectedly. Financial stress could have destroyed many relationships, but not theirs. Instead of hiding his vulnerability, Diego was open about his fears.

"I'm scared," he had told Sophia one evening, his voice tremblir "I've always defined myself by my work, and now I feel lost."

60

Sophia's response was a testament to their trust. She didn't try to fix everything or minimize his feelings. Instead, she simply held his hand and said, "We'll figure this out together. Your worth isn't defined by a job title."

Her belief in his character remained unshaken. She saw beyond the temporary setback, recognizing his resilience, creativity, and potential. This unwavering support gave Diego the emotional safety to be vulnerable, explore new career paths, and grow.

Deepening Through Shared Vulnerability

They learned to:

- Rely on each other's emotional strengths
- Share concerns openly
- Celebrate small victories together
- Face challenges as a united team

Their conversation shifted to reflect on the trust they had built. Diego had recently been offered a challenging new job that would require significant personal growth. In the past, he might have hesitated to take such a risk. Now, bolstered by Sophia's consistent support and their mutual trust, he felt empowered.

"I trust that even if I fail, you'll see me," Diego said. "Not as a failure, but as someone trying his best."

Sophia's response embodied their shared commitment. "Always," she replied. "Your attempts, your struggles, your successes—they're all part of who you are. And I'm here for all of it."

Their trust wasn't just about surviving challenges—it was about creating a space where both could be authentically themselves. They had cultivated a relationship where:

- Emotional safety was paramount
- Each person's character was deeply respected
- They believed in each other's good intentions
- Their commitment was a daily, active choice

This trust changed their relationship from a simple partnership to a strong collaboration. Their bond showed that trust is more than just being reliable. It's about creating a space for unconditional support. In this environment, both people can grow, succeed, and evolve.

Their story illustrates the broader truth that trust enhances every aspect of a relationship. When mutual purpose aligns, when genuine attraction draws individuals together, and when communication flows freely, trust naturally deepens, making connections resilient and transformative.

Diego and Sophia's relationship showed that trust isn't a destination—it's a continuous journey of choosing each other, day after day, with openness, vulnerability, and unwavering belief in one another's potential.

Three Elements Of Trust

Trust is a must in any strong relationship. Trust is what transforms acquaintances into confidants and colleagues into allies.

Trust is not just about believing in someone's capacity to act but also in their intentions and character. Trust stems from believing in the reliability, truth, ability, and integrity of another. Trust is when you feel emotionally safe with someone, evident by what you share with them, and they with you. When trust is present, relationships can withstand trials and flourish. Trust is demonstrated by what you both say and do.

In chapter 16 we will discuss in detail the three levels of trust. Until then, you can start to understand and build the following three characteristics of trust that permeate all levels of trust and build meaningful relationships:

1. Reliability/Competence

Reliability forms the foundation of trust through consistent behavior. To strengthen reliability in your relationships:

- **Consistent follow-through:** Do what you say you'll do when you say you'll do it.
- **Transparent communication:** Share information openly, especially when plans change.
- **Time commitment:** Invest regular, quality time in relationships that matter.
- **Mutual accountability:** Hold yourself to the same standards you expect from others.

2. Emotional Safety

Emotional safety creates an environment where vulnerability and authenticity can thrive. To build emotional safety:

- **Freedom to be vulnerable:** Create safe spaces for sharing fears, failures, and joys. This allows people to open up without worrying about rejection, betrayal, or harmful gossip.
- **Acceptance of imperfection:** Embrace the humanity in yourself and others rather than demanding flawlessness.
- **Understanding without judgment:** Listen to understand before forming opinions or offering solutions.
- **Space for growth:** Allow people to evolve without holding their past against them.

3. Respect

Respect acknowledges what values and abilities each person brings to the relationship. To display respect:

- **Recognition of abilities:** Actively acknowledge the unique strengths others contribute.

- **Respect for expertise:** Value others' knowledge and experience in their areas of strength.
- **Support for development:** Encourage growth through opportunities and constructive feedback.
- **Belief in potential:** Trust not just who someone is today, but who they're capable of becoming.

Reflecting on the deep connection between Sophia and Diego, we see that the culmination of their shared journey was based on a common purpose and mutual respect for each other's abilities and qualities. However, as they navigated through various challenges and celebrated successes together, a profound trust developed between them. This trust wasn't instantaneous; it was cultivated over time through consistent, open communication and a shared commitment to their cause. It became the reason to be confident of their partnership, allowing them to take greater risks and push boundaries in their endeavors.

The evolution of Sophia and Diego's relationship illustrates how trust, built over time, can solidify a connection and empower you, me, and those in our circles to achieve remarkable feats together. Their experience mirrors the broader truth that trust enhances every aspect of a relationship. When purpose aligns, when attractiveness (in all its forms) draws individuals together, and when communication flows freely, trust naturally follows. It is trust that deepens these connections, making them resilient and enduring.

How do you get that level of trust in your relationships? The way we communicate, along with congruency in our actions, can greatly help with this…along with time. Be patient and committed. Like Sophia and Diego, you can build a foundation of trust that can support the weight of your shared dreams and aspirations.

Reflection Exercise

Consider your strongest relationships:
- What specific actions built trust?
- How was trust tested and strengthened?
- What makes you feel safe to be vulnerable?
- How do you demonstrate trustworthiness?

Sophia and Diego's relationship demonstrates how trust, built gradually through consistent actions and shared commitment, creates a foundation strong enough to support ambitious dreams. Their story continues to evolve, each new challenge and success adding another layer to their foundation of trust.

Practical Application

- Start small and be consistent
- Acknowledge and learn from mistakes
- Communicate openly about expectations
- Celebrate shared successes
- Allow trust to develop naturally

———————— *KEY TAKEAWAYS* ————————

Within the principles of P.A.C.T., trust is the element that cements and strengthens all other aspects of a relationship. Sam and Alex's journey from colleagues to champions of a cause encourages us to invest in building trust in our relationships, understanding its pivotal role in creating bonds that are both meaningful and lasting.

Trust is the last key part of a P.A.C.T. It helps form strong relationships with the people who matter most. Trust acts like a stronghold, where lasting connections can grow. As you strive to build trust in your relationships, remember the importance of alignment in purpose, appreciation of authenticity, attractive communication, and the role of time in strengthening trust. Together, these elements form the pillars of relationships, or a pact, with others that not only survive but thrive.

PART THREE

Toxic vs Attractive Communication

Words hold immense power—they can heal or harm, connect or divide. In this essential section, we'll uncover the hidden patterns of toxic communication that undermine our relationships and contrast them with attractive communication that fosters trust and understanding. You'll learn to identify destructive habits like judgment and shame, and gain the tools to replace them with empathetic, constructive dialogue. This is where you'll begin to transform not just the way you speak, but how you truly connect with others.

Communication:
The Language of Connection

Every skill has its masters, but sometimes wisdom comes from unexpected sources. My journey to understanding the true essence of communication began in an unlikely place—the Deaf community. Deaf people know something about communication that most hearing people do not. What I learned from them transformed the way I connect with others.

At age 30, I encountered a profound teacher in the form of circumstance. My friend's youngest daughter, Ariana, was experiencing progressive hearing loss. When her family embraced ASL and Deaf culture, I joined them. I didn't know this journey would change how I saw communication and its role in human connection.

What followed was an experience in mastering a true fundamental of communication—one that traditional training had never provided.

The Picture Perfect Definition

My ASL mentor shared a definition of communication so powerful in its simplicity that it has stayed with me for decades:

"Communication is taking the picture in your mind and creating that same picture in another person's mind." In all my life, I've never heard a better definition of communication.

This definition transcends language:

- In ASL, hands paint pictures in the air.
- In spoken language, words create mental images.
- In writing, descriptions form visual scenes.
- In body language, movements tell emotional stories.

Example of Clear Communication

Two people seeing the same picture in their minds:

Think about when someone says, "We're on the same page." What they're really expressing is, "We're seeing the same mental picture." When everyone involved shares a clear, unified understanding, they are more likely to take action. They are also more likely to feel seen, understood, and validated.

Beyond Words

Why is this definition of communication so impactful? Because traditional definitions often fall short. Take this common definition of communication: "The imparting or exchanging of information or news." While technically accurate, it strips communication of its depth and nuance. It's like describing a dance as simply "the movement of feet in patterns."

While I love my ASL mentor's clear and succinct definition of communication, there is a bit more to it. The Britannica Dictionary expands on this idea by defining communication as "the process of using words, sounds, signs, or behaviors to express or exchange information." Now we're getting somewhere. Communication isn't just verbal—it's a symphony of:

- Spoken words
- Body language
- Facial expressions
- Tone and inflection
- Physical presence

Most people instinctively think of words as the primary way of communicating. What's interesting about Britannica's definition is that it broadens communication to include non-verbal forms as well. Signs, body language, facial expressions, actions—all of these convey and express information.

Studies show that more than 50% of communication is non-verbal. Essentially your voice-box is the smaller part of communication. A 1970s study by psychologist Albert Mehrabian breaks it down like this:

- 55% of communication is body language (facial expressions, posture, gestures, etc.)
- 38% is tone of voice (inflection, pitch, speed, etc.)
- 7% is the actual words spoken.

By receiving verbal and non-verbal communication, we can create a clearer picture in our mind, tying back to the original succinct definition of communication mentioned earlier.

Can you imagine how much more effective your message is when you've mastered both verbal and non-verbal communication to create clear pictures in others' minds? After all, a picture is worth more than 1,000 words.

When communication works:

- Understanding flows naturally
- Actions align with intentions
- Relationships deepen
- Trust builds organically
- Influence grows naturally

But what happens when there is miscommunication? It is the exact opposite–someone sees a different picture than what was actually intended.

Example of Miscommunication

Two people seeing different pictures in their minds:

Miscommunication kills connection, undermines trust, and derails any positive intentions behind communication. While we try our best to be clear, when our mental pictures don't align and miscommunication occurs, everything changes:

- Connection breaks
- Trust erodes
- Influence diminishes
- Relationships strain
- Goals remain unmet

The Goal of Communication

Communication can serve many purposes, but when it comes to creating and attracting authentic relationships, there's one main goal: to make everyone feel seen (acknowledged), heard (understood), and validated. In short, the goal is to foster connection.

Think about your most satisfying interactions. They are likely the ones where you felt:

- Truly understood
- Deeply acknowledged
- Genuinely validated
- Completely heard
- Authentically connected

Genuine communication goes far beyond the dry definition of "expressing or exchanging information." The exchange of information must have a purpose. To achieve this, you speak to a person's heart—their values, purpose, and beliefs that motivate them.

A New Definition

Combining these insights, we can define communication as: *"The process of creating shared mental pictures through words, sounds, signs, and behaviors, to build trust, foster connection, and create positive influence."*

Looking Ahead:
The Two Faces of Communication

Once you understand the fundamental nature of communication—creating shared mental pictures—it's crucial to recognize that this power can be wielded in two different ways.

In the next chapter, we'll explore Toxic Communication—patterns and habits that distort our mental pictures and damage connections. Through Sam and Alex's ongoing story, we'll see moments where miscommunication could have derailed their partnership and learn how to recognize and avoid these traps.

Consider these scenarios:

- A well-intentioned comment that causes unexpected hurt
- A message lost in emotional translation
- Words that build walls instead of bridges
- Patterns that slowly erode trust

But understanding toxic communication is only half the journey. In Chapter 12, we'll explore Attractive Communication—the art of creating clear, compelling mental pictures that deepen connection and build lasting influence.

As we move forward, remember: Every interaction is an opportunity to either strengthen or strain our connections. The choice lies in how we craft and share our mental pictures.

——————————— *KEY TAKEAWAYS* ———————————

This chapter reveals the profound insight that true communication is "taking the picture in your mind and creating that same picture in another person's mind." Moving beyond traditional definitions focused merely on exchanging information, we've explored how effective communication creates shared understanding through multiple channels—both verbal and non-verbal.

When our mental pictures align, connection flourishes, trust deepens, and influence grows naturally. Conversely, miscommunication fractures relationships and undermines our goals. At its core, meaningful communication serves one fundamental purpose: to make others feel seen, heard, and validated—to create a genuine connection.

Before moving forward, take a moment to reflect on your most recent significant conversation. Did you successfully transfer the picture in your mind to the other person? Or did you encounter resistance, confusion, or disconnect?

Today, commit to one conversation where you consciously focus on creating clear mental pictures. Before speaking, visualize exactly what you want the other person to understand. Pay attention not just to your words, but to your body language, facial expressions, and tone. After your conversation, ask yourself: Did they see what I intended them to see? This practice, of consciously creating shared mental pictures, will begin transforming your relationships immediately.

Every interaction is an opportunity to either strengthen or strain our connections. The choice lies in how we craft and share our mental pictures. The communication masters understand this secret: connection happens not when we speak, but when we are truly understood.

Toxic Communication:
The Language of
Unhealthy Relationships

T he words left her mouth before she could stop them. "I'm so sorry for being late. My father passed away unexpectedly last night." Ashley's voice trembled slightly as she spoke into the phone—the phone her manager Omar had deliberately put on speaker for the entire grocery store to hear. How would you have responded to Ashley if you were her manager? Omar, as we will soon find out, responded with toxic communication.

So, what exactly is "Toxic Communication"? **Toxic communication refers to words and expressions that subtly instill shame, judgment, or selfishness.** It rarely comes with a warning label and often sneaks into conversations, disguised as honesty or concern.

What makes toxic communication so dangerous is not just its impact, but its invisibility to those who use it most. "Straight shooters" and those who pride themselves on "telling it like it is" often leave behind a trail of fractured relationships, completely unaware of the harm they've caused.

By understanding toxic communication, we can learn to recognize it—both in others and in ourselves. This awareness allows us to address it right away and keep the P.A.C.T. in our relationships strong. In the following chapters, we'll dive deeper into the core components of toxic communication: judgment and shame. We'll explore how to spot these harmful patterns, not just in others, but within ourselves—because the most dangerous poison is the one we don't realize we're serving.

To start, let's look at a real-life example of toxic communication in action through the story of Omar and Ashley, and begin recognizing how these patterns manifest.

Omar vs Ashley

Ashley managed the dairy section at a local grocery store. She was super friendly and kind, with a warmth that made everyone feel welcome. Plus, she worked hard, always showed up on time, and cared a lot about doing her job well. But then, one day, she suddenly quit. She didn't give a two-week notice or anything. She just left and never came back.

Why would someone as engaging and hardworking as Ashley leave her job like that? It's often the same reason many people leave their jobs: a bad relationship with their boss. In this case, her boss was Omar. Omar had a way of using hurtful words to try to control his employees, including Ashley.

Omar, known for his blunt approach to management, noticed Ashley's unusual delay one morning. Opting for a public confrontation, he called her on speakerphone, allowing the entire store to become an audience to their private conversation.

With a heavy heart, Ashley began to share her circumstances, her voice trembling slightly. "I'm so sorry for being late, Omar.

My father passed away unexpectedly last night," she disclosed, her words heavy with sorrow. "Between trying to handle this, and moving with my two kids and boyfriend, it's been overwhelming." Her attempt to maintain composure under such scrutiny was both admirable and heart-wrenching.

Omar's response, intended to offer sympathy, came across as uncomfortably insincere. "Ah, that's tough, Ashley. Really tough," he said, his voice lacking the depth of genuine empathy. "But, you know, we all have jobs to do. Can't let personal stuff get in the way." The starkness of his reply, especially given the gravity of Ashley's situation, struck a discordant note with everyone who overheard.

Despite Omar's clumsy attempt at consolation, his focus swiftly returned to the inconvenience Ashley's absence had caused. "We're strapped without you here. It makes things hard for everyone," he continued, his tone more accusatory than understanding.

This interaction, broadcasted for the entire store to hear, laid bare the underlying issues in their working relationship. Omar has a habit of driving people away. He tends to use toxic communication to try and manipulate his employees. Omar thinks it's hard to find good workers because, in his view, people don't want to work hard or be dependable. But the real reason it's tough for him to keep workers isn't what he thinks. He keeps losing staff because of how he speaks to them. He keeps losing his staff because he has a relationship with them that is hurtful and insensitive.

This incident, though brief, was a profound revelation for Ashley. It highlighted the lack of support and empathy at work. This made her challenges even harder, both in her job and in dealing with personal tragedy. Witnessed by employees and customers alike, the conversation became a turning point for Ashley, signaling the end of her time at the grocery store. Faced with an environment that no longer supported her growth or well-being, she made the difficult decision to leave.

Toxic communication pushes people away, as we saw with Ashley and Omar because it creates an emotionally unsafe environment where others feel they can't trust their true thoughts and emotions with you. It's often easy to recognize when others are using toxic communication, but harder to notice when we're doing it ourselves. Since we're not always aware of our own words, we're frequently surprised by reactions that don't align with our intentions.

Why don't we always notice when we're using toxic speech? The simple answer is that we're not taught to recognize it. In some cultures, this type of communication is even viewed as powerful or cool. Think about certain famous personalities in TV shows, movies, or politics. Their harsh words might attract some followers, but they can also create division and alienate others.

For example, very blunt people often end up pushing more people away, despite their pride in being the kind of person who "tells it like it is" or is a "straight shooter." The truth is, wealth, fame, and power don't guarantee healthy relationships. Omar's story is proof of this—his success couldn't shield him from the consequences of toxic communication.

KEY TAKEAWAYS

In this chapter, we've delved into the concept of toxic communication—language patterns that unnecessarily evoke feelings of shame, judgment, and selfishness in our relationships. Through Ashley and Omar's story, we've seen how even well-intentioned words can create deep rifts between people when delivered without empathy or awareness.

Toxic communication works like an invisible barrier, slowly dismantling connections while often going unnoticed by those who use it most frequently. We've learned that being "blunt" or "telling it like it is" might seem like virtues in certain contexts, but these approaches often mask harmful communication habits that push people away instead of bringing them closer.

The most dangerous part of toxic communication is not seeing our role in it. Cultural norms, media portrayals, and our upbringing can make harmful speech patterns seem normal. These patterns can become so ingrained that we don't notice the damage they do. As we saw with Omar, this blindness keeps us stuck in a cycle. We blame others for relationship failures instead of looking at our own communication habits.

Today marks your opportunity to break this cycle of toxic communication. Before reading the next chapter, commit to these two actions:

1. Identify Your Toxic Triggers: The first step in breaking the cycle is recognizing what situations cause you to slip into judgmental or shame-inducing language. Is it stress, feeling disrespected, or something else? Understanding these triggers is the key to defending yourself against toxic communication.
2. Cultivate Awareness: Awareness is the antidote to toxic communication. The relationships you save through more conscious communication may be some of the most important in your life. Start noticing when toxic patterns appear, and take a step back before responding.

In Chapter 11, we'll address how to break free from toxic communication patterns and in Chapter 12, we'll turn tap into the power of attractive communication—language that builds connection rather than erodes it. Until then, let's dive deeper into understanding the components of toxic communication, so we can effectively avoid these patterns moving forward.

9

Judgment: Closing Minds, Connection, and Collaboration

"**T**hat dress is much too flashy for a family event like this, don't you think?"

With those eleven words, Aunt Mary transformed Emma's moment of joy into an experience of shame. The colorful dress that had made Emma feel bright and confident moments before now felt like a glaring mistake. As relatives chuckled around her, Emma's smile faded, replaced by burning cheeks and a desperate wish to disappear into the background.

All it took was one judgment.

We've all been Emma, proudly wearing our colorful dresses or nice suits. Our ideas and true selves shine brightly. Then, someone judges us and our confidence vanishes in an instant. If we're honest, we've all been Aunt Mary as well, sharing opinions on others' choices without seeing how our words affect them.

Judgment is often the silent relationship killer that masquerades as helpful feedback, honest opinion, or even moral clarity. In reality, it's often the language pattern that closes minds fast, creating invisible walls between people who might otherwise connect deeply.

What makes judgment so dangerous is how normalized it has become in our culture. We celebrate the "straight-shooters" and admire those who "don't hold back," often without questioning whether their bluntness serves connection or destroys it. We mistake strong opinions for strength of character, failing to recognize that true strength lies in holding space for different perspectives.

Judgment: "Deciding that an action or motive of something, someone, or a group, is right, wrong, good, or bad."

This simple definition helps clarify the destructive power of judgment in our most important relationships, especially when it's negative. When we judge, we don't just evaluate actions—we create distance. We don't merely express opinions—we close the door to understanding. And most critically, we don't just share preferences—we damage trust.

Judgment can be especially hard to navigate in relationships. Sometimes, actions are clearly wrong—like stealing candy from a store. Almost everyone agrees that stealing is bad. But what about situations like Emma's? If Aunt Mary dislikes Emma's dress, but Aunt Carol loves it, who's right? Is Aunt Mary's opinion more valid than Aunt Carol's? And if one is right, does that automatically make the other wrong?

This illustrates how judgment can easily cloud our ability to understand, respect, and connect with others. It's not always about right or wrong—it's about creating space for different perspectives and avoiding judgments that create unnecessary conflict.

This shows how tricky judgment can be. We naturally value our own opinions—sometimes more than those of others. This can lead to arguments about who's right and who's wrong as if our opinions are facts. But really, they're just preferences, and arguing about them can hurt our connection and damage our emotional trust with others.

Remember, our opinions aren't facts. Keeping an open mind helps us stay away from being too judgmental. Being curious instead of judgmental is a better approach. It's one of the 3 C's of Attractive Communication, which we'll address later. If Aunt Mary had been more curious about why Emma chose her dress, she might have understood better and not judged so quickly.

In this chapter, we'll explore how judgment infiltrates our personal and professional relationships, often without our awareness, and how it systematically dismantles the connection we work so hard to build with others. Through stories like Emma's embarrassment and others you'll soon discover, we'll learn to recognize judgment in its many disguises and develop the skills to choose. Now, let's explore how judgment can shape our personal lives.

Judgment in Your Personal Life

Here's an illustrative example: Every time Mike helps around the house, like folding the laundry or tidying up, his wife, Lisa, inspects his work and says, "This is how you fold the clothes? Let me show you the right way." Her words are clear and direct, leaving no room for doubt that she finds Mike's efforts inadequate. Mike feels discouraged; his attempts to contribute are consistently criticized. He starts questioning his ability to perform even simple tasks correctly. This ongoing correction makes Mike hesitant to help out, fearing that anything he does will be deemed wrong or not good enough. His initial enthusiasm fades, replaced by a reluctance born from the fear of judgment.

Mike and Lisa's story shows how small comments can hurt deeply. When Lisa criticizes how Mike folds laundry, it doesn't just make him feel inadequate; it makes him doubt his ability to help. Mike thinks being a good husband means supporting Lisa by pitching in at home. Lisa's ongoing judgments shake this belief. Now, he feels like he's failing not just at chores but also as a partner.

This is the ripple effect of judgment. Repeatedly speaking in a judgmental way can profoundly impact how someone feels about themselves and their willingness to continue helping. For Mike, it wasn't just about the laundry; it was about feeling valued as a husband who genuinely wanted to support his wife. When we're not careful with our words, we can unintentionally make someone feel unimportant and discouraged.

Instead of immediately criticizing Mike's method, Lisa could have approached the situation with curiosity. She could have said, "I noticed you fold the clothes differently than I do. Can you show me why you like to fold them that way?" This might seem small, but leading with curiosity can prevent toxic language from sneaking into relationships. By asking Mike about his method, Lisa creates an opportunity for them to share their perspectives without judgment. This approach fosters learning, mutual respect, and a deeper connection, strengthening their relationship and their P.A.C.T.

Judgment in relationships often shows up when partners evaluate each other's actions, decisions, or preferences as right or wrong, good or bad. This can strain the relationship and hinder emotional intimacy. By choosing curiosity over judgment, we can build stronger, more understanding connections. Here are some typical ways judgment shows up:

1. Critiquing Daily Choices: Criticizing someone's choices in everyday matters—such as their style, food preferences, or how they spend their free time—can make them feel that their personal preferences are wrong.

2. Questioning Decisions: Doubting or questioning your partner's decisions—whether regarding their career, finances, or social interactions—can make them feel that their judgment isn't trusted or valued.

3. Dismissing Feelings: Telling someone they're overreacting or their feelings are unjustified is a form of judgment invalidating their emotional experience.

4. Correcting Household Tasks: Like in the story of Mike and Lisa, criticizing how chores are done, from laundry to cooking, can make a partner feel unappreciated and hesitant to contribute.

5. Disapproving of Interests or Hobbies: Showing disapproval or mocking someone's hobbies or interests can make them feel that their passions are not valued or accepted.

6. Blaming During Arguments: Consistently assigning blame to someone for most problems or disagreements can make them feel as though they are always in the wrong.

7. Public Correction or Embarrassment: Correcting someone or pointing out their flaws in public can lead to feelings of shame and judgment.

Avoiding these behaviors is crucial for maintaining a healthy, supportive relationship where both people feel valued and respected for who they are. When people feel valued and respected, trust grows and the P.A.C.T becomes stronger and happier.

Judgment in Your Work and Social Life

In professional settings, judgment can be equally devastating:

"That's not how we do things here," a manager tells a new employee offering fresh ideas. This simple phrase carries judgment that can stifle innovation and enthusiasm.

At work, the lunchroom conversation turned serious when the topic of vaccines came up. Alex mentioned quietly that he was still deciding about getting the vaccine, hoping to have a thoughtful discussion. But Jamie, sitting across the table, loudly said, "What's there to think about? Only selfish people don't get vaccinated. You're not one of those, are you?" Everyone at the table went silent, glancing between Jamie and Alex. Alex felt his face heat up with embarrassment as he became the sudden focus of the room. Though Jamie might have thought he was standing up for what was right, his words made Alex feel attacked and judged for his hesitation. The judgment in Jamie's voice made Alex question his place among his coworkers, transforming what could have been a supportive conversation into a moment of deep discomfort and doubt.

The story shows how quickly a conversation can turn uncomfortable when someone makes a strong judgment about what others should do, like getting a vaccine. Jamie's loud comment made Alex feel bad for just sharing his thoughts. This teaches us that being too quick to judge can hurt people's feelings and make them feel left out or wrong.

A better way for Jamie to respond could have been with curiosity instead of judgment. Jamie could have asked, "I'm curious, Alex, what concerns do you have about the vaccine?" This would have allowed Alex to express his feelings without fear of judgment, while Jamie could have shared information in a supportive way to help Alex feel more confident in his decision. Being curious helps everyone understand each other better and keeps the conversation friendly and open.

In social dynamics, statements of judgment often surface in various ways, affecting relationships and overall team morale. Here are some common scenarios where people might express judgement, keeping in mind the earlier definition of judgment as deciding whether someone's actions or motives are right or wrong, good or bad:

1. Performance Feedback: When feedback focuses on what went wrong or criticizes without offering constructive ways to improve, it can feel like a personal judgment rather than helpful guidance.

2. Work Style Differences: Critiquing someone's approach to a work project because it differs from one's own, suggesting that there is only one "right" way to achieve results.

3. Decision Making: Questioning others' decisions in a manner that implies they were not thought through or were incorrect, without giving them a chance to explain their reasoning behind them.

4. Professional Choices: Making disparaging remarks about someone's career path, choice of projects, or professional interests as if their choices are inferior.

5. Interpersonal Skills: Offering criticism of someone's communication style or the way they engage with others in social or professional settings, in a way that suggests their interpersonal skills are lacking or flawed.

6. Work–Life Balance: Judging colleagues based on how they balance work and personal life, such as making assumptions about commitment or productivity based on how much overtime they work.

7. Innovation and Ideas: Dismissing new ideas or innovative approaches prematurely, indicating a belief that traditional methods are always better.

8. Personal Life Choices: Bringing personal biases into the workplace by making judgmental statements about aspects of a colleague's life that don't impact their work performance or way of life.

To foster a positive and supportive workplace, it's critical to recognize and address these judgmental dynamics. Encouraging open-mindedness, understanding, and constructive communication can create an environment where everyone feels valued and respected.

──────────── *KEY TAKEAWAYS* ────────────

Judgment in relationships can be a tricky road to navigate because we often hold our opinions in high regard, sometimes valuing them over others'. This can lead to debates about who's right and wrong, mistaking personal preferences for facts. Such arguments can harm our P.A.C.T. with those around us. It's important to remember that opinions aren't facts. Embracing curiosity over judgment fosters a more open and understanding communication style, known as one of the 3 C's of Attractive Communication. For instance, if Aunt Mary had been more curious about Emma's choice of dress, she might not have judged so quickly.

The situation between Mike and Lisa highlights how even minor negative comments, such as criticism over folding laundry, can deeply impact someone's self-esteem and willingness to help. This kind of criticism challenges their core beliefs about their role and value in the relationship or team. By focusing on positive reinforcement and sharing knowledge in a supportive way, we can transform everyday tasks into opportunities for connection and growth.

Addressing judgmental behavior in both romantic and professional relationships is essential for creating a supportive environment where everyone feels valued and respected. Preventing the damaging effects of judgment not only strengthens your P.A.C.T. but also deepens trust, fostering greater connection and happiness.

Next, let's dive into shame to better understand what it is and how it can hinder our communication and erode our relationships. Judgment and shame are closely intertwined, much like thunder and lightning—one often follows the other.

10

Shame: The Trust Destroyer

Brené Brown gave a great definition of shame in her book Braving the Wilderness. She writes: 'Shame: "The feeling of being small, unworthy, flawed, never "good enough."'

Shame differs from guilt. Guilt says "I did something bad," while shame says "I am bad." It's the feeling of being fundamentally flawed or unworthy.

Shame appears in communication in various forms:

- Direct criticism ("You always mess this up")
- Comparative statements ("Why can't you be more like...")
- Public humiliation ("Let me show everyone how it should be done")
- Dismissive responses ("Whatever, just let me do it")

The story of Mike and Lisa from earlier illustrates how shame operates in relationships:

Mike decided to help with household chores, starting with laundry. Lisa's response? "This is how you fold clothes? Let me show you the right way." Her words carried an implicit message: you're not even capable of basic tasks.

The impact was profound. Mike stopped helping around the house, not because he didn't want to contribute, but because every attempt led to criticism that made him feel inadequate.

Sarah's experience is another example of how shame happens, and its impact on connections and relationships.

During the school talent show, Sarah decided to sing, her voice trembling with nerves. Later, Mark, attempting to be funny in front of his friends, loudly joked that her singing sounded like a cat caught in a rainstorm. Sarah laughed along, but her smile didn't quite reach her eyes. Later, when she thought no one was watching, Sarah folded her song lyrics. She tucked them deep in her backpack, wanting to hide them forever. She tried to act like Mark's actions didn't hurt, but her silence told a different story. She avoided singing out loud, even to her favorite songs.

This is an example of how toxic communication evokes shame. The feelings of being small, unworthy, flawed, and never "good enough" were exactly what Sarah experienced after Mark's mocking comment. She felt like she would never be good enough for the school talent show, not now and not ever.

In the story of Ashley and Omar mentioned in chapter 8, we see shame is what Omar made Ashley feel as if she was failing as an employee despite grieving circumstances.

Let's explore how shame can appear in your personal and work life. Then, we'll explore how to address and correct situations where you might unintentionally cause someone to feel shame.

Shame in Your Love Life

Lisa and Tom sat quietly at dinner. Suddenly, Tom said, "You always burn the toast, just like you mess up everything else." Lisa laughed and replied, "I guess cooking isn't my superpower." Later, when Tom wasn't looking, she tossed away the new recipe book she had bought. A little voice inside her whispered that maybe she wasn't good at anything, not just cooking.

Tom's words felt harmless and were meant as a joke. Still, they made Lisa think she was always doing something wrong. Even though she tried to laugh it off, she couldn't shake the feeling that she wasn't enough, no matter how hard she tried.

Shame in relationships, particularly within the context of a partnership or marriage, can be evoked through various behaviors and communications. Shame can also be evoked in the smallest ways, as Tom did to Lisa. While Tom was trying to be funny, it caused Lisa to feel shame.

It's important to recognize these patterns as they undermine the foundation of trust and respect that healthy relationships are built upon.

Here are common ways a spouse might evoke shame in their partner. Have you ever experienced any of these in your relationships?:

1. Criticizing Their Choices: Making negative comments about their interests, career, or daily decisions.

2. Dismissing Their Successes: Downplaying or mocking their achievements, making them feel insignificant.

3. Embarrassing Them in Public: Calling out mistakes or flaws in front of others, causing humiliation.

4. Comparing Them to Others: Suggesting that someone else is more attractive, intelligent, or successful, making their partner feel inadequate.

5. Invalidating Their Feelings: Ignoring, belittling, or making fun of their emotions, making them feel foolish for expressing themselves.

6. Controlling or Isolating Them: Dictating their actions or limiting their social connections, leading to feelings of entrapment and loneliness.

7. Controlling or Isolating Them: Dictating their actions or limiting their social connections, leading to feelings of entrapment and loneliness.

8. Constantly Bringing Up Past Mistakes: Repeatedly reminding them of past failures, preventing healing and growth.

9. Undermining Intimacy: Making them feel unwanted or unattractive, especially in moments of closeness.

10. Withholding Affection as Punishment: Deliberately withdrawing love, kindness, or affection to make them feel unworthy or ashamed.

Doing these things would make anyone feel small and emotionally wound their partner. It's important to notice if any of these behaviors occur in your relationship. If you notice that you sometimes commit any of these behaviors, change them quickly because everyone deserves to feel loved and respected in a relationship.

Shame in Your Workplace

During the team meeting, Kevin eagerly shared his idea for the new project, but Mark quickly responded with a laugh, "Oh, not another one of Kevin's 'brilliant' plans. Remember how well the last one went?" Everyone chuckled, and Kevin said with a forced smile, "Right, I'll try to come up with something better." But for the rest of the meeting, Kevin stayed silent, not offering any more of his usual creative ideas. Later, sitting alone at his desk, Kevin quietly closed the notebook filled with his ideas and slid it into his drawer, feeling like maybe his contributions weren't valuable. Mark's harsh words, meant to be funny, left Kevin questioning his place in the team and his confidence in his ideas.

In a workplace, sometimes people can make others feel shameful about themselves or their work. Doing so not only drives people away, hinders good relationships, it also inhibits people from showing up as the best possible version of themselves. This will hurt the team's overall performance and happiness at the workplace. It weakens the connection and trust that all relationships need to flourish.

Here are some common ways this can happen. Which ones do you recognize at your workplace?

1. Making Fun of Mistakes: Laughing at someone when they make a mistake or do something wrong, instead of helping them learn how to do it right.

2. Talking Down About Ideas: Saying that someone's ideas are always bad or silly can make them afraid to share new ones.

3. Ignoring Their Hard Work: Not saying "thank you" or "good job" when someone works hard on something can make them feel as if their work doesn't matter.

4. Leaving Them Out: Excluding someone from meetings, emails, or lunch groups can make them feel isolated and like they don't belong.

5. Comparing Them to Others: Telling someone they should be more like someone else at work, making them feel like they're not good enough the way they are.

6. Being Mean About How They Talk or Look: Making fun of the way someone speaks, dresses, or looks, making them feel bad about themselves.

7. Telling Them They're Always Wrong: Consistently insisting someone is wrong, even when they're not, can cause them to doubt themselves.

8. Taking Credit for Their Work: Receiving praise or recognition for work that was actually done by someone else, making them feel invisible and unappreciated.

9. Giving Them Only the Hardest or Most Undesirable Work: Always making them do the jobs that nobody else wants or are the most difficult, making them feel like they're only there to do the tough stuff.

10. Not Listening to Them: When they try to talk or give an opinion, act like what they're saying isn't important, making them feel like their thoughts don't matter.

Doing these things can make someone feel small and damage productive work dynamics. It's essential to treat everyone with kindness and respect at work, so everyone can feel good and do their best.

──────── *KEY TAKEAWAYS* ────────

Assess your communication, especially when it comes to shame. Is this part of your communication habits, whether personally or professionally? If you ever say or do something that makes your partner, friend, or coworker feel bad, avoid statements like, "Why are you like that?" or "That's not right." These kinds of comments imply that their feelings are wrong.

Instead, listen to how they feel and acknowledge those emotions out loud. It's more effective to truly understand their feelings and reflect that understanding back to them. This shows that it's safe for them to feel how they do and that you genuinely care about their emotions. By doing so, you help avoid triggering feelings of shame and preserve—or even strengthen—the quality of your P.A.C.T.

11

The Cost of Toxic Communication and How to Break Free

"**D**oes your boss ever give you any positive feedback?" I asked my friend. He touched his chin, his eyes drifting upward as if searching his memory.

"No, not for months," he admitted. "All I hear is what I'm doing wrong and why my way is never right."

My friend, once enthusiastic about his job, now feels constantly on edge, as if his position is at risk. The boss he once respected and had a great relationship with has become a source of stress, chipping away at his confidence and motivation. He used to look forward to learning from a supportive mentor. Now, he avoids his boss to escape constant criticism, judgment, and shame.

Toxic communication isn't just hurtful in the moment, but also damaging over time. A harsh comment may seem small, but its effect adds up and can be devestating. Each judgment, shame, or selfish act erodes trust. This creates emotional walls between people.

Over time, these small hurts can change a strong bond into a tense, distrustful one.

A small communication issue can grow into a serious problem if ignored. Toxic communication makes it hard for people to open up. It stops them from taking risks or showing who they really are. It creates an unsafe atmosphere where individuals feel misunderstood and uneasy, undermining their emotional well-being. Relationships built on such foundations become weak. Once trust is broken, it's even harder to rebuild.

The Immediate and Long-Term Effects of Toxic Communication

The impact of toxic communication goes far beyond the immediate sting of harsh words or judgments. Consider the following effects:

1. Reduced Communication: When people feel judged or criticized, they begin to withdraw. Conversations become more surface-level, as individuals fear being misunderstood or hurt. This withdrawal over time leads to emotional isolation, cutting off one of the most vital components of connection: meaningful dialogue. Without open communication, relationships stagnate, and individuals grow further apart.

2. Increased Defensive Reactions: Toxic communication often triggers defensive responses as individuals try to protect themselves from further emotional harm. Instead of engaging in open, honest conversations, people may shut down, withdraw, or lash out. These defensive reactions create a cycle of mistrust and disconnection, as people prioritize self-protection over genuine connection.

3. Lost Opportunities for Connection: Every conversation is an opportunity to build trust, share understanding, and strengthen bonds. Toxic communication steals these moments, replacing them with missed opportunities for deeper connection. When we are defensive or closed off, we miss the chance to engage with others on a more meaningful level, whether in professional settings or personal relationships.

4. Diminished Collaboration: In both personal and professional relationships, collaboration is the key to success. But toxic communication undermines our willingness to cooperate. If individuals feel their ideas are ridiculed, their efforts dismissed, or their feelings invalidated, they become less likely to contribute or work together towards a shared goal. This diminishes creativity, increases frustration, and perpetuates a toxic cycle that leaves everyone feeling disconnected and unproductive.

5. Damaged Self-Esteem: Over time, toxic communication chips away at an individual's self-worth. Constant exposure to criticism, sarcasm, or judgment can lead people to doubt their abilities, question their value, and feel inadequate. The emotional scars left by such interactions can be deep, often leading to diminished self-esteem, anxiety, and even depression. This erosion of self-worth can affect both the individual and their relationships.

As these toxic communication patterns continue, the consequences grow more severe. The person who endures this harmful behavior may start to believe these messages. Over time, this can lead to emotional abuse, a form of harm that slowly chips away at a person's confidence, mental health, and ability to trust others.

The Emotional Abuse of Toxic Communication

Though toxic communication may not always appear as direct verbal abuse, its long-term effects can mirror those of emotional abuse. Dr. John Gottman's research has identified communication patterns that consistently indicate a decline in relationships. These patterns include criticism, contempt, defensiveness, and stonewalling. Psychologist Michael Johnson's studies further demonstrate how these nonphysical forms of abuse, including undermining behaviors and toxic communication patterns, can cause psychological harm comparable to more overt forms of abuse. Constantly undermining a person's feelings, thoughts, or behaviors with toxic words or actions wears down their emotional resilience. The psychological damage is often subtle but profound: feelings of worthlessness, diminished trust in others, and a pervasive sense of isolation.

Over time, the person on the receiving end of toxic communication may feel as if they're walking on eggshells—constantly worried about triggering negative reactions. The fear of being criticized or belittled can lead to chronic stress, anxiety, and depression. Emotional depletion affects not only the individual on the receiving end but also those around them, as they become more withdrawn and less engaged.

This is exactly what happened to me. If you remember from the opening chapter, I felt like a failure as a husband and began withdrawing from my friends. I grew more silent at home, no longer sharing my true passions or concerns as openly as I once did. Why? Because recent experiences taught me that I would be punished by the people closest to me if I shared my personal thoughts or chased my goals. It's a terrible feeling, one I hope you never have to experience. But if you can relate, there is hope! You can break free from the effects of emotional abuse.

It's crucial to recognize that emotional abuse can occur in any type of relationship—romantic, familial, professional, or even friendships. If left unaddressed, toxic communication can cause lasting damage to one's mental health, self-esteem, and ability to form healthy, trusting relationships.

Breaking Free from Toxic Communication

The first step in breaking free from toxic communication patterns is recognizing them. Once we identify how these patterns manifest in our relationships, we can begin to take control and shift the dynamic toward healthier, more constructive communication.

Simply stopping toxic behavior isn't enough; we must replace harmful communication patterns with healthier, more effective practices. This requires intentionality, self-reflection, and a willingness to be vulnerable. It's about fostering communication that builds trust, opens hearts, and nurtures mutual respect.

Here are practical strategies for transforming toxic communication into healthy, constructive dialogue:

Instead of judgment, practice curiosity:
- "Tell me more about your choice."
- "What led you to make that decision?"
- "Help me understand your perspective."

By replacing judgment with curiosity, we create an environment where the other person feels heard and understood, rather than criticized or dismissed.

Instead of shame-inducing statements, offer support:
- "I appreciate your effort."
- "Let's figure this out together."
- "What would make this easier for you?"

Offering support in moments of vulnerability helps the other person feel valued and reinforces a sense of emotional safety, encouraging deeper connection.

Instead of selfish responses, show empathy:

- "That sounds really challenging."
- "How can I help?"
- "What do you need right now?"

Empathy fosters trust by showing that we care about the other person's feelings and are willing to be present for them, rather than prioritizing our own needs or agenda.

Lessons for Change

Breaking free from toxic communication requires both self-awareness and actionable steps. These key lessons will help you shift toward healthier, more constructive interactions that foster trust and connection.

- **Understand Toxic Communication Patterns:** Recognizing harmful communication styles—such as judgment, shame, and selfishness—is essential for breaking free from them.
- **Build Healthy Boundaries:** Establishing emotional boundaries helps prevent toxic communication from taking hold. Boundaries allow us to protect our mental and emotional health while maintaining healthy relationships.
- **Realize Small Changes Lead to Big Results:** Even small adjustments in how we communicate—such as being mindful of tone, listening actively, and showing empathy—can have a profound impact on our relationships.
- **Embrace Awareness and Practice:** Breaking toxic communication patterns requires both awareness of our behaviors and consistent practice of healthier communication strategies. This is an ongoing process, not a one-time fix.

- **Remember, the Goal Isn't Perfection, But Progress:**
  Striving for perfect communication is unrealistic. However, progress is possible with small, consistent efforts to be more mindful and intentional in how we engage with others.

KEY TAKEAWAYS

Understanding toxic communication patterns is key to breaking free from them and establishing healthy boundaries in how we communicate. As we've seen, toxic communication blocks connection by undermining emotional safety and trust in relationships. In the next chapter, we'll dive into the alternative: Attractive Communication, and explore the 3 C's framework, which can transform the way we connect with others.

Remember:

- Every interaction is an opportunity to either build or break trust.
- Small changes in how we communicate can lead to profound effects.
- Breaking toxic patterns requires both self-awareness and intentional practice.
- The goal isn't perfection, but progress.

As you move forward, think about how you can apply these insights to your personal and professional relationships. What communication patterns do you notice? Where can you make small adjustments for a significant impact?

The journey from toxic to attractive communication begins with awareness and continues with conscious choice. In the next chapter, we'll explore how to make these choices consistently and effectively.

12

Attractive Communication and the 3 C's

Attractive Communication: "Demonstrating warmth and competence in communication that makes people feel acknowledged, understood, and validated."

Attractive Communication is built on three key principles, known as the 3 C's: **Curiosity, Clarity, and Courtesy.** These three elements help us avoid Toxic Communication, serving as a powerful tool for effective and respectful dialogue. By using the 3 C's, we ensure that both we and those we communicate with feel understood, respected, and valued.

Attractive Communication is a bridge that helps us share our thoughts and build trust—what we call our P.A.C.T. It allows us to be seen, heard, and validated. It also creates space for others to feel the same. By embracing these principles, we can enhance our relationships and achieve more of what we truly want in life.

Chapters 8-11 explained Toxic Communication—what it is, how it shows up in our conversations, and why we must avoid it. Now, we shift to a more vital topic: how to communicate to strengthen emotional safety, satisfaction, and connection in relationships. This approach is called Attractive Communication. It's essential for building genuine connections where everyone feels supported and their needs are met.

For example, Ella and Jordan had been dating for three months, enjoying dinners out and long walks together. However, when they decided to host their first dinner party as a couple, they hit a snag over what menu to serve. Ella wanted a fancy Italian feast to impress their friends, while Jordan thought a casual barbecue would be more fun. This disagreement threatened to dampen their excitement for the party, but they remembered the 3 C's of Attractive Communication: Curiosity, Clarity, and Courtesy.

Jordan showed Curiosity by tactfully asking Ella, "Can you tell me what you like about an Italian feast that would be perfect for our party?" Instead of dismissing her idea, he listened carefully as Ella explained her vision of creating a warm, elegant evening. This made Ella feel heard and appreciated, deepening their connection.

Ella laid out her ideas for the Italian menu, explaining each dish she wanted to prepare. Jordan, in turn, shared his thoughts on why a barbecue could be more relaxing and enjoyable for their friends. By showing genuine curiosity, Jordan listened attentively to Ella's perspective and asked thoughtful follow-up questions. In turn, Ella reciprocated, engaging with Jordan's ideas and vision for the party. Both of them communicated their points clearly, making it easier for the other to understand their reasoning.

Although Ella and Jordan disagreed, they spoke kindly. They used phrases like, "I love your idea, and I wonder if we could incorporate this too." This kept their planning positive and collaborative. They maintained a supportive, open dialogue the whole time.

Using the 3 C's of Attractive Communication, Ella and Jordan solved their menu issue. They also built mutual respect, trust, and understanding. Together they created an Italian-themed party. Their friends loved the casual vibe. Their skill in handling the disagreement with curiosity, clarity, and courtesy brought them closer. This showed them how attractive communication can turn challenges into chances for creative solutions and growth in their relationship.

KEY TAKEAWAYS

- Attractive Communication is rooted in warmth and competence, helping people feel acknowledged, understood, and valued.
- The 3 C's—Curiosity, Clarity, and Courtesy— are essential tools for building trust and emotional safety in any relationship.
- Curiosity invites open dialogue by showing interest in the other person's thoughts, feelings, and perspective.
- Clarity helps prevent misunderstandings by expressing ideas in a way that's thoughtful, honest, and easy to follow.
- Courtesy ensures kindness and respect stay at the center of every interaction—even during disagreements.
- Practicing Attractive Communication transforms potential conflicts into opportunities for connection, creativity, and authentic collaboration.
- Communicating this way doesn't just resolve issues—it builds stronger, more resilient relationships over time.

13

Lead With Curiosity: Opening Minds and Hearts

C uriosity is more than just asking questions—it's about genuinely seeking to understand others' perspectives, feelings, and experiences. It's an expression of empathy, which is crucial for building meaningful connections in relationships. Curiosity is also the antidote to judgment and the foundation for true connection.

You may have heard the saying, "Curiosity killed the cat." Often, it's used to discourage asking questions or showing too much interest in others' affairs. But when it comes to building relationships, curiosity isn't just safe—it's essential.

If there's one thing I hope you take away from this book, it's this: Lead with curiosity. Curiosity is the first of the 3 C's that make up Attractive Communication. Unlike the cautionary tale of the cat, curiosity in relationships won't harm you. Instead, it can prevent Toxic Communication and stop frustration and anger before they even begin. I've seen countless times how starting conversations with curiosity can:

- Help shy people open up
- Get stuck conversations moving again
- Bring out new ideas and solutions
- Calm down tense situations

In my fitness career, I frequently encountered individuals who were nervous about joining a group fitness class, especially those who were overweight, out of shape, or new to the experience. Their nerves often made them shy and quiet. As a coach, it was my responsibility to create a comfortable and welcoming environment for them.

One such person was Jennifer. In her first class, she was shy and quickly left afterward. But with each subsequent class, she began to open up more. Over time, she grew so comfortable that she found it hard to leave after class! Eventually, Jennifer shared with me, "I love these classes because you make me feel welcome. I've become proud of doing my best, and I've even made new friends here."

It was incredible to see her transformation from a shy, reserved individual to a confident and friendly fitness enthusiast!

I've only seen positive outcomes from people who carefully start with curiosity.

So, what is curiosity, and what does it mean to lead with it?

Curiosity is wanting to learn or know more about something. When you lead with curiosity, you ask questions because you legitimately want to understand better or discover something you didn't know before.

Take for example the story of Ella and Jordan mentioned earlier. Curiosity was key in preventing toxic communication and fostering a creative solution.

When Jordan asked Ella about her love for Italian food, he showed genuine curiosity. This approach created a space for understanding instead of conflict. It helped avoid negative reactions that could easily arise from dismissing each other's ideas. Plus, it led to a creative solution that satisfied them both.

Leading with curiosity can transform potential disagreements into opportunities for innovation and agreement. By genuinely listening to others' perspectives with an open mind, you too can uncover new solutions never seen before. Consider another example:

In a marketing office, a team faced a tough challenge: their latest ad campaign wasn't catching on, and the deadline was fast approaching. Sarah, the team leader, suggested doubling down on social media ads, but Mark, a newer member, hesitated. Instead of shooting down his concerns, Sarah asked, "Mark, what's on your mind about the social media plan?" This simple question opened the door to a deeper conversation.

Mark shared his observation that their target audience spent more time on podcasts than social media. At first, Sarah was skeptical, but her curiosity led her to ask more about Mark's idea. Together, they explored the potential of advertising on popular podcasts related to their product.

This shift in strategy, born from Sarah's willingness to be curious rather than dismissive, transformed the campaign. The podcast ads struck a chord with their audience, increasing engagement far beyond what the original social media ads had achieved.

Sarah's curiosity not only prevented a breakdown in communication, which could have led to frustration and wasted efforts but also uncovered a strategy that was more aligned with their audience's habits. The team's ability to pivot to podcast advertising demonstrated how staying open and curious can lead to better solutions not previously revealed or readily apparent to the team, reinforcing the value of every team member's input and fostering a culture of collaboration and innovation.

Struggles In Leading With Curiosity

Reading these stories it might seem easy to be curious and open in our conversations. However, many people find it hard to start with curiosity. Why is that? One big reason is the fear of feeling exposed. Being curious can reveal not only new or hidden ideas but also mistakes and misunderstandings in what we currently think or feel. Many worry that if their ideas or feelings are perceived wrongly, they might face judgment and shame from others. This fear of vulnerability can make people worried about losing their status, respect, or influence among their peers.

So, instead of asking questions and being curious, some people choose to stay quiet, acting like they don't care, or they stubbornly stick to their ideas, refusing to listen to others. These actions hinder the development of trust in a P.A.C.T., which is crucial for fostering strong, happy relationships and having a positive influence. Trust grows when people feel listened to, understood, and valued while being dismissive or stubborn erodes it.

Even though being open might feel risky, the chances of being met with shame and judgment are pretty low according to science. According to the book *Nonviolent Communication*, by Marshall Rosenberg, people are more likely to respond well to genuine curiosity. People tend to like it when someone is genuinely interested in them and their thoughts. This kind of exchange makes it more likely for others to listen, understand, and value your ideas in return. This back-and-forth helps build stronger trust in your authentic relationships and helps everyone achieve shared goals.

It's also crucial to understand that curiosity must be genuine to be effective. If you approach it merely as a "communication tactic," it will come across as inauthentic to your audience. They'll sense you're just "checking a box" (see Chapter 5, under "Why Traditional Training Fails"). As a result, people will either tell you what they think you want to hear or avoid sharing anything at all.

If you're curious just so you can "win" an argument, the other person will notice. They may become defensive. This will damage trust and connection, damaging the relationship. When you lead with curiosity, be sure to validate the other person's view rather than trying to prove them wrong.

Curiosity and the Circle of Trust

Curiosity is more than just a conversational tool. It's a smart and strategic way to navigate human connections. When we show real curiosity, we make a safe space. This space lets people open up their Circle of Trust (See Chapter 18 about The Circle Of Trust).

By asking thoughtful, open-ended questions, we invite others to move from their Public Trust Circle—where interactions are surface-level and guarded—to their Private Trust Circle, where more meaningful sharing becomes possible.

This approach is closely tied to the Purpose element of P.A.C.T. Curiosity allows us to uncover the underlying motivations, values, and driving forces that shape a person's core purpose. When you engage in conversations with genuine curiosity, you're not just collecting information—you're seeking to understand the deeper essence of another person's goals and beliefs. Curiosity becomes a powerful bridge between external interactions and internal truths, enabling you to connect on a level far beyond casual conversation. By demonstrating a willingness to listen and understand, you create a safe space for others to share their true selves, gradually building trust and deepening their own Circle of Trust.

Asking Curious Questions

When it comes to curiosity, not all questions are created equal. Some questions open minds, while others close them. Let's explore some strategies for using curiosity-based questions and statements to deepen connection, open minds, and build collaboration.

The Power of "What" and "How"

The most effective curious questions typically start with "what" and "how." These question starters invite exploration rather than defense:

- "What led you to that conclusion?"
- "How did you come to that decision?"
- "What would an ideal solution look like to you?"
- "How might we approach this differently?"

You might wonder: "Why not use questions that start with who, when, or where?" There's nothing wrong with those questions—they're often necessary for gathering specific information. Questions like "Where did this happen?" or "When is the deadline?" have a purpose. However, if you want people to open their minds to new perspectives or elaborate on their thoughts and feelings, "what" and "how" questions create the space for deeper sharing.

The Problem with "Why"

"I don't understand. What's so bad about asking 'why'?" This is a fair question. We've been asking "why" since we were barely old enough to speak. For decades, it's been our go-to way to express curiosity and seek understanding.

Yet as adults, "why" questions are often perceived more as interrogations than expressions of genuine curiosity, regardless of our intentions. Many people use "why" questions to get others to see what they perceive as obvious faults in thinking or behavior:

- "Why did you forget to call me?"
- "Why would you make that decision?"
- "Why don't you ever listen?

When we ask "why," we may unintentionally prompt the other person to become defensive, as they feel the need to justify their decisions. Defensiveness, by nature, closes people off, like a fence around a home. Instead, we want to encourage openness—like a door that invites new possibilities and understanding. Asking "why" often achieves the opposite of what we intend, causing the other person to become defensive. However, there is one effective use for "why" questions: when someone has done or said something you agree with. In these cases, asking "why" allows them to reinforce their reasoning, strengthening the alignment between you both.

The Magic of Similes

Using simile-based statements allows you to share your perspective without it being received as judgmental. Phrases like:

- "It seems like..."
- "It looks like..."
- "It sounds like..."

Starting phrases with similes is also known as labeling. Labeling is different from judgment. Judgment is like a court room verdict. Judgment makes definitive statements such as "That is...". Labeling, on the other hand, presents your understanding as an observation rather than a verdict, keeping the other person's mind open and curious. Smiles and labels create an opportunity for clarification without adding unnecessary tension, as you'll see in this real-life situation with my former client, Martha.

Martha and Raquel

Martha's experience with her girlfriend Raquel illustrates common communication pitfalls, and how applying the principles stated earlier in this chapter can significantly reduce relationship tension. Martha was one of my clients who was constantly arguing with her girlfriend, Raquel. Martha wanted to spend more time with Raquel, and it seemed like Raquel was resistant to doing so.

Martha's initial approach to discussing quality time with Raquel perfectly illustrates a common communication pitfall. When frustrated by their lack of dates, she would typically ask, "Why don't you care to spend time with me?" While this might seem like an attempt to understand, the question forces Raquel into a defensive position. By using a "why" question, Martha inadvertently created tension, compelling Raquel to justify her actions rather than engage in a collaborative conversation.

What Martha truly wanted was a deeper understanding and a path forward. She learned to change her approach by leading with curiosity and empathy. By reframing her concern to "I want to spend time with you on a real date. It seems like (notice the use of simile) work has gotten you tired recently. How can we be more consistent for date night?" Martha created an entirely different dynamic. Martha used a simile ("It seems like...") to focus on "how" instead of "why." This approach helped her avoid toxic communication that feels accusatory and judgmental. Instead, she invited Raquel into a conversation where both could help find a solution. The result was collaborative problem-solving, not defensive justification. This created a chance for a genuine connection.

Follow these three recommendations—emphasize "what" and "how" questions, use similes, and save "why" for positive reinforcement—and you'll be amazed at how people will feel emotionally safe discussing anything with you.

For an in-depth discussion on questions and statements that effectively build empathy and connection, I recommend *Never Split the Difference* by Chris Voss (see 'Recommended Reading' at the end of this book).

——————————— *KEY TAKEAWAYS* ———————————

Curiosity often gets a bad rap from the old saying, "Curiosity killed the cat," suggesting it's better to keep to ourselves. However, when it comes to building strong connections, or P.A.C.T.s, being curious is key. This means that instead of avoiding questions about someone's thoughts or feelings, we should dive in and ask more. As long as we are having this conversion when all parties are emotionally grounded, asking curious questions isn't just safe; it's necessary.

Embracing curiosity can prevent misunderstandings and hard feelings, opening the door to better conversations and relationships. It turns out that asking questions and authentically wanting to understand people leads to good outcomes. It can make someone who's usually quiet feel comfortable to talk more, help stalled conversations flow again, find new solutions to old problems, and even make tense moments calm.

Curiosity is all about wanting to know or learn something more. Leading with curiosity means starting conversations with questions that show you want to understand or uncover something new. This approach doesn't just help avoid negative communication; it promotes positive interactions. By being genuinely interested in others, we create a welcoming space for open and honest dialogue. This not only helps our conversations but also strengthens our P.A.C.T.s, making our relationships happier and more fulfilling.

The next time you are seeking a deeper connection or understanding of someone, try being curious first before assuming understanding. Clarity is a superpower for gaining understanding and avoiding misunderstandings. In the next chapter, we will dig into the second "C" of Attractive Communication: Clarity.

Clarity:
Changing Misunderstandings
to Understanding

C larity isn't just about being clear in what we say—it's about ensuring mutual understanding and validation. It's the difference between hearing words and comprehending their meaning. Remember our definition of communication: taking the picture in your mind and creating that same picture in someone else's mind.

When clarity fails, miscommunication occurs, creating two different pictures and potentially damaging relationships.

Few things are more frustrating in communication than when there is miscommunication. Consider Lena and Jake's discussion:

Lena and Jake were working on a group project. One afternoon, while discussing their project's direction, Jake made a comment that Lena found hurtful and a bit offensive. Her first instinct was to respond sharply, convinced Jake was in the wrong. However, remembering the importance of leading with curiosity, Lena took a deep breath and chose a different path.

"Jake, can you help me understand what you meant by that comment?" Lena asked, her tone both gentle and firm. With this simple question, she led with curiosity while seeking clarity, creating space for dialogue rather than confrontation. Jake, momentarily caught off guard, reflected on his words and saw how they might have been misunderstood. He clarified his thoughts, explaining that his intention wasn't to offend but to express concern about a specific part of the project they had yet to finalize.

Lena chose to ask for clarification instead of letting conflict grow. This choice helped them understand each other's viewpoints better. They moved forward with their project, now more aware of how to share ideas respectfully. Through curiosity, Lena and Jake turned a tricky situation into a chance for growth. This strengthened their teamwork and their P.A.C.T.

On the flip side, miscommunication can harm our connections, reputation, and good intentions, just like it nearly did for Lena and Jake. Clarity prevents miscommunication and makes others feel seen, heard, and validated. We can avoid misunderstandings by communicating and understanding clearly. If we pause to ask a curious question, we clarify thoughts and feelings. This helps maintain a happy relationship with the other person.

Common Mistakes to Avoid in Conveying Clarity

Sometimes we think we're being clear when we're not. Remember when Lena's first instinct was to respond sharply to Jake's comment? Why? She was initially convinced that she fully understood what Jake meant and believed he was wrong. Fortunately, Lena led with curiosity and asked for clarity before verbalizing her shaming and judgemental thoughts.

A common mistake is saying "I hear you" and thinking it suffices. This phrase isn't bad or wrong, but it rarely, if ever, helps achieve our goal. The goal is for the other person to feel seen, heard, or validated. Instead, the phrase "I hear you" often comes across as dismissive of what the other person said, or neutral at best. Can you recall a time when someone said, "I hear you"? Did you instantly think, "Whew! I completely believe you now, and I feel truly understood"? Probably not. More likely, you felt the urge to explain yourself further.

If you often react this way and want others to feel understood, try summarizing their response. This shows you are listening and really understand them. When they feel heard, they might say, "That's right." This shows they feel validated. There is something even more damaging than only saying "I hear you," and that's adding "but" after "I hear you." This is something we've probably all done, and it damages trust in our P.A.C.T.

Saying "I hear you, but..." sends the message that we aren't listening or that we don't value the other person's opinions, thoughts, or feelings. I once heard it said that the word "but" immediately conveys dismissal of whatever was said before it. This can quickly erode trust in our P.A.C.T. People may start feeling that they can't share their authentic thoughts or feelings because they fear dismissal, which can lead to shame and judgment. As a result, they may withdraw from communication, or the conversation may become tense.

By using curiosity alongside clarity, we maintain trust and ensure mutual understanding. Together, these two elements prevent misunderstandings, allowing everyone to feel seen, heard, and validated. This strengthens our P.A.C.T.s, fostering healthier, happier relationships.

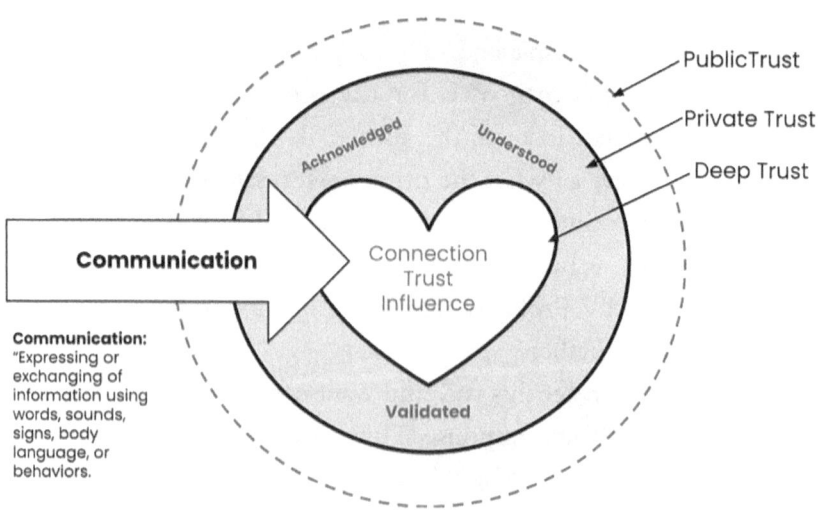

You might be wondering if saying "I hear you, but" doesn't provide clarity, what does? Labeling emotions and summarizing what someone has said helps them feel heard and validated. This approach is much more effective than simply saying, "I hear you."

Clarity Technique #1: Labeling

When someone expresses strong emotions, labeling those emotions in your response helps them feel seen and heard, creating an immediate sense of connection. To soften the impact, use similes like "sounds like," "looks like," or "seems like," as explained in the previous chapter. For example, Jake used this approach when he said, "It seems like you're frustrated." This ensures that your label doesn't come across as harsh judgment, even when acknowledging emotions that might be seen as negative. Using similes yields one of two beneficial outcomes:

1. Confirmation: "That's right"—making the person feel immediately understood (as with Lena)
2. Clarification: They correct or refine your understanding, revealing a more accurate perspective

Both results strengthen your connection, perspective, and mutual understanding.

Benefits Beyond the Moment

Labeling emotions benefits both parties. When you acknowledge someone's feelings:

- They feel genuinely seen and understood
- Trust develops more naturally
- They become more willing to share their authentic thoughts and feelings
- The relationship grows through mutual respect

The Beauty of Imperfect Labels

But what if you don't get the label right? As a fitness trainer, over the years I have regularly opened conversations with emotional observations—often incorrectly! On one occasion, I greeted my client Juan with "Looks like you're having a great day." He responded: "Not really. It's been tough. I'm just happy not to be at work right now." With Brittany, I asked "Tough day?" and she explained: "No, I'm just lost in thought. This is my resting face when I'm contemplating."

These "mistakes" rarely, if ever, offend anyone. They often lead to deeper conversations that help clarify what's truly going on. It's not about perfect accuracy but rather showing, "You are worthy of my attention, and I'm genuinely trying to connect with you." Plus, people often enjoy correcting misperceptions and opening up even more. Whether they appreciate that you noticed their feelings or are eager to share their true emotions, the result is the same: increased openness, emotional clarity, and an appreciation for your attentiveness.

Beyond Difficult Moments

Don't reserve labeling only for tense situations. The goal of attractive communication is always to make others feel seen, heard, and validated. Try labeling positive emotions too—acknowledge someone's excitement or joy when they share good news. Watch how they light up when you recognize their enthusiasm. These moments strengthen your P.A.C.T., showing that you're a trusted presence in both difficult conversations and moments of celebration.

Clarity Technique #2: : Summarizing

Summarizing is exactly what it sounds like—providing a concise statement of the main points. Notice the impact it had when Lena used this with Jake:

After Jake shared why he wanted a different approach for their project, Lena paused to think about it.. She then summarized his points, saying, "So, it sounds like you think a different approach might help our project stand out more, and you're focused on doing something unique, right?" Hearing his thoughts echoed back to him, Jake felt a sense of relief. Additionally, using a simile softened the tone, preventing it from sounding judgmental and making the statement more likely to be received well. This also gave Jake the space to edit the summary if needed.

Lena's act of summarizing and reflecting Jake's thoughts back to him demonstrated that she truly listened and understood his perspective. It made Jake feel valued and heard, shifting the conversation from tension to collaboration. Both of them felt more aligned in their purpose and project goals, setting the stage for better teamwork.

The next time someone shares their thoughts or experiences with you, use summarizing as a tool to make them feel seen and heard. Like labeling, summarizing typically leads to one of two outcomes:

1. They'll respond with something like, "That's right," and feel seen and understood.
2. They'll correct your understanding, providing clarity to any misperceptions or revealing hidden truths.

Does Validating Mean that We Agree?

One common concern when validating others is the fear of being misunderstood as agreeing with something we don't actually agree with. So, how can you validate someone's thoughts, opinions, or feelings when you don't share the same perspective?

This is where the power of labeling and summarizing comes in. When we label or summarize someone's feelings and statements, we're not implying agreement. Instead, we're conveying, "I understand how you reached this conclusion and why you feel this way." We're not labeling their thoughts as right or wrong, good or bad—we're simply acknowledging their perspective. In essence, labeling and summarizing show that we recognize the validity of their emotions and thoughts, without judgment.

—————————— *KEY TAKEAWAYS* ——————————

Clarity is essential in communication. It means ensuring that both what we say and how we understand others are completely clear, so there's no room for confusion. Without clarity, we can't effectively support the people we socialize or work with. It's also impossible to show or feel understanding and validation. Demonstrating clarity is a way of showing that we truly understand where someone is coming from and that we respect their feelings and thoughts.

However, sometimes we think we're being clear when we're not, or we might fail to express ourselves in a way that shows we genuinely understand. Simply saying "I hear you" isn't enough to make someone feel truly listened to. Adding "but" after "I hear you" can make matters worse—it can sound like we're dismissing their feelings or implying their opinion isn't important. This damages the trust and emotional safety in the relationship, making it harder for people to open up with us.

By using clarity and curiosity together, we can prevent misunderstandings and ensure everyone feels seen, heard, and valued. This not only reduces arguments but also strengthens our relationships and enhances happiness. When we communicate clearly and show a genuine effort to understand others, we build trust. People trust us with their thoughts and feelings. This builds our P.A.C.T.s—our shared promise to support and listen to each other's purpose. This helps us get along better with everyone around us.

15

Courtesy and Tact: Say What You Mean Without Being Mean

When you think of being polite, you likely picture holding the door open for someone or saying "Please" and "Thank You." But courtesy in communication goes beyond these basic gestures—it's about being mindful of how our words and actions affect others while still staying authentic and honest. Courtesy, or tact, involves avoiding unnecessary offense and showing respect in how we communicate. Here's an example of tact in action:

At a local community center, a group of friends gathered for their weekly book club. This week, they had read a popular mystery novel that had everyone talking. When it came to sharing thoughts, Jenna eagerly awaited feedback, enthusiastic about every twist and turn of the story. Alex, known among friends for his straightforward opinions, was about to critique the plot's predictability in his usual direct manner. However, he remembered the club's rule about keeping discussions positive and constructive. He took a moment, then said, "Jenna, I love how excited you were about the book's mystery elements. I also love good plot twists. "For our next book, I'd be open to one with more unexpected twists—it seems like we'd all enjoy the excitement of a story that keeps us guessing." Jenna smiled, grateful for Alex's considerate approach and thoughtful suggestion. This moment highlighted the power of tact. Alex shared his honest opinion in a way that encouraged Jenna and maintained a light, engaging atmosphere in the book club. Instead of Alex blurting out his negative opinion of the book, he chose his words carefully, sharing his honest thoughts without hurting Jenna's feelings. It's possible to be both honest and kind when we think about how we say things.

It's important to emphasize that courtesy, or tact, at its core, means avoiding unnecessary offense. This involves speaking kindly and showing appreciation when someone shares something personal with us. It's about not unintentionally hurting others' feelings. Without tact, we risk damaging the emotional safety needed for building strong relationships. Words can quickly become harmful, rather than fostering understanding and kindness.

Think of blunt words like hot sauce or hot peppers, and courtesy like sugar. While some people enjoy the heat and prefer more directness, language without tact can be uncomfortable, like swallowing too much spice. Others need words to be a bit sweeter. To ensure our words are well-received and don't unnecessarily upset anyone, we need to use tact in the way we communicate.

You might think, "But I like to be spicy. That's just who I am, and I'm not changing for anyone. I keep it real." If that's the case, consider the role of curiosity. Being curious and open to adjusting how we communicate helps us connect with people who might be different from us. When they're curious too, they'll also strive to understand you better. This creates a balance—while you aim for clarity, they offer grace, even if your words come across as a bit "spicy" to them. Just like a skilled chef tailoring a meal to an audience, you can craft your words to be more palatable, no matter who you're talking to.

It's important to understand that being courteous doesn't mean avoiding the truth or softening it to the point of inaccuracy. You don't have to water down the facts or sugarcoat them—that's not respectful. The truth can be tough, and sometimes it's not what we want to hear. But courtesy allows us to deliver hard truths without unnecessary harshness, ensuring others don't feel more ashamed than the truth itself might make them feel. Being courteous means being honest, but doing so in a way that is respectful and compassionate.

Equally important as speaking with courtesy is listening with courtesy. What does this mean? Just as we strive not to needlessly offend, we should also avoid assuming negative intent too quickly. True courtesy extends beyond our words—it shapes how we listen and interpret others as well.

Tact helps us handle tough conversations. It keeps us from being too harsh and helps us not take offense quickly. Instead, we strive to communicate with both clarity and kindness, even when delivering a difficult message. This approach fosters open, constructive, and emotionally safe conversations, even when the topic is challenging.

In the end, being courteous helps others listen and understand you better. It also makes it easier for you to understand them. This increases the chances of a positive outcome for everyone. Isn't it worth adjusting your approach just a little to make that happen? You don't have to change who you are—just tailor how you express yourself depending on the situation.

The Story I'm Making Up Is...

A simple phrase can turn a potentially explosive conversation into one of connection. I learned this firsthand in what I now call "The Great Kitchen Towel Standoff."

In our narrow galley kitchen, barely wide enough for two people to pass each other, I noticed a bright red kitchen towel on the floor. This struck me as odd, as my wife is typically the neater one between us. Assuming she'd been in a rush, I tossed the towel into the washing machine.

The next day, another kitchen towel appeared in the same spot. My suspicions grew. "This can't be coincidental," I thought. "She must be testing me to see how long I'll let it sit there." I despise these kinds of tests. Instead of asking her about it, I hypocritically decided to experiment to see how long it would take her to pick it up.

Five days passed. Shockingly, the towel remained unmoved.

I knew I needed to address it, but how? My first instinct—"Why are you testing me with this kitchen towel?"—would sound accusatory if I was wrong. Even asking, "Why have you left that kitchen towel there for days?" would place all the blame on her when I could've easily picked it up myself. Either way, it seemed like a conversation bound for conflict.

Fortunately, I had recently heard a psychologist on a podcast share a communication technique she used with her husband. When upset about something she perceived he was doing intentionally, she would begin with: "The story I'm making up in my mind is…"

This phrase acknowledges that our perceptions may not align with reality—even when we're convinced they do. It invites curiosity instead of confrontation.

So, I decided to give it a try. Sitting down with my wife, I said, "I've noticed the kitchen towel on the floor for days. The story I'm making up in my mind is that you're testing me to see how long it takes before I pick it up. I imagine this because you're cleaner than I am, and you've sometimes expressed frustration about always being the one who cleans."

Her response? A chuckle that quickly turned into genuine laughter. "I honestly didn't even notice the towel on the floor," she admitted. "I've been completely exhausted after work and haven't been paying attention to the house."

What could have escalated into an argument became a meaningful talk about her work stress and how I could better support her. We ended up bonding more deeply that day. Combining courtesy with curiosity through that simple phrase created an opportunity for us to connect.

Next time you find yourself certain about someone else's intentions, try starting with, "The story I'm making up in my mind is..." It stops you from approaching the conversation as an adversary and invites mutual understanding instead.

Practical Application of the 3 C's

To implement Attractive Communication effectively, consider these practical strategies:

1. To foster *Curiosity*:
- Ask open-ended questions
- Respond with labeling and summarizing
- Show genuine interest in others' perspectives
- Seek to understand before being understood

2. To create *Clarity*:
- Reflect back what you've heard
- Check for understanding
- Use specific, concrete language
- Address misunderstandings promptly

3. To cultivate *Courtesy*:
- Choose words thoughtfully
- Consider timing and context
- Balance honesty with sensitivity
- Acknowledge others' feelings

The Impact of Attractive Communication

When we consistently apply and practice the 3 C's, we create an environment where:

- Trust flourishes naturally
- Connections deepen organically
- Conflicts are resolved more easily
- Innovation flows freely
- Emotional safety is protected

Remember Ella and Jordan's dinner party? Their skillful communication not only resolved the immediate challenge they faced but also strengthened their relationship, better preparing them for future challenges.

─────────── *KEY TAKEAWAYS* ───────────

Courtesy and tact are essential components of effective communication that go beyond basic politeness. They involve considering how our words impact others while remaining authentic and honest. This chapter emphasizes how we can communicate truthfully without causing unnecessary offense—striking a balance between the "spice" of directness and the "sweetness" of consideration.

The powerful technique of saying, "The story I'm making up in my mind is..." exemplifies how combining courtesy with curiosity can transform potentially confrontational conversations into opportunities for a deeper connection. This approach acknowledges that our perceptions may not align with reality, creating space for mutual understanding rather than conflict.

Begin using courtesy in your daily interactions. Choose your words thoughtfully. Be aware of timing and context. Balance honesty

Courtesy and Tact: Say What You Mean Without Being Mean

with sensitivity. Begin with low-stakes conversations and observe how this approach enhances your relationships. Before your next challenging conversation, ask yourself: "How can I express this truth clearly while respecting the other person's feelings?" Remember, communicating with tact doesn't mean sacrificing honesty; it means delivering the truth in a way that can be genuinely heard and appreciated.

The journey to mastering Attractive Communication is ongoing, but each step brings you closer to more meaningful, fulfilling relationships. In the next chapter, we'll explore how to choose your relationships wisely and apply these principles to build and maintain connections that truly matter.

PART FOUR

Your Communication Transformation

Knowledge transforms into wisdom through practice. This section goes beyond theory to offer practical tools for transforming your personal communication. You'll uncover the secret behind charisma, master the art of vocal tone, and develop a more nuanced approach to interpersonal dynamics. These chapters serve as your toolkit for becoming a more effective, authentic communicator—one who can navigate complex social and professional situations with grace and confidence.

The Secret Fourth C: Charisma

Take a moment to think about the most charismatic person you know. Maybe it's a captivating actor, an inspiring leader, or that magnetic family member who lights up every gathering. If you asked a room full of people this question, you'd likely hear a wide range of answers. Yet while charisma is instantly recognizable, few can clearly define what makes someone charismatic.

Now, here's something even more revealing: ask those same people if they consider themselves charismatic, and most will quickly say, "No." This immediate denial highlights a common misconception about charisma—that it's an innate, almost mystical quality reserved for the exceptionally charming or influential.

Even the dictionary definition doesn't offer much clarity. Merriam-Webster defines charisma as "compelling attractiveness or charm that can inspire devotion in others." No wonder so many people assume they don't have it! This definition makes charisma sound like an exclusive trait of movie stars and world leaders. If someone doesn't see themselves as particularly attractive, charming, or inspiring, they're unlikely to believe they possess charisma at all.

But what if everything we've assumed about charisma is wrong? What if charisma isn't a rare, inborn trait but a skill—one that anyone can develop?

The Truth About Charisma

Vanessa Van Edwards, best-selling author and founder of People School, offers one of the clearest definitions of charisma in her book *Cues:Master the Secret Language of Charismatic Communication.* What makes her definition so powerful is its simplicity. She defines charisma as *"the balanced display of warmth and competence."*

This definition changes everything. Instead of viewing charisma as a rare, magical trait for only a few people, we can now view it as a real skill that we can develop. According to Van Edwards, charismatic people are likable, trustworthy, capable, and memorable. All of these qualities stem from their ability to balance warmth and competence.

Take a moment to reflect—do you come across as both warm and competent? Most people naturally lean more toward one than the other. However, real impact happens when you find the right balance. It doesn't have to be a strict 50/50 split. You can express both qualities in a way that fits your personality and situation.

The Imbalance Problem

Charisma breaks down when there's an imbalance between warmth and competence. People who struggle with charisma typically fall into one of three categories:

1. They display too much competence but not enough warmth.
2. They display too much warmth but not enough competence.
3. They fail to display enough of either.

Let's examine the first two pitfalls more closely.

The Competence-Heavy Leader

A person who leans too heavily on competence without warmth often comes across as rigid, unapproachable, or even arrogant. While they may be highly respected for their abilities, they struggle to build strong personal connections.

Consider Marcus, a brilliant software architect at a leading tech company. His technical skills were unmatched—he could solve complex coding problems in minutes, where others took hours. His reputation for excellence preceded him, and his managers trusted him to deliver results.

But Marcus had a problem. Despite his expertise, his team was falling apart. Over the past year, three talented developers had requested transfers, and two had quit outright. During his performance review, his manager, Sarah, had to address the elephant in the room.

"Marcus," she began carefully, "your technical skills are exceptional. But I've noticed some concerning patterns in how you interact with the team."

She shared the feedback she'd received: Marcus regularly dismissed others' ideas without consideration, spoke condescendingly during code reviews, and made junior developers feel inadequate for asking questions. During meetings, he would impatiently tap his fingers while others spoke, making it clear he saw their contributions as a waste of time.

"I know you care about quality," Sarah continued, "but your approach is crushing team morale. Being right isn't enough if no one wants to work with you."

Marcus is a perfect example of what happens when competence isn't balanced with warmth. While he was trusted for his technical skills, his lack of warmth made him unapproachable. This weakened his ability to lead effectively. His story is similar to Omar's from earlier chapters demonstrating how skill without kindness can hurt relationships and team dynamics.

The People-Pleasing Problem

On the other end of the spectrum, individuals who display too much warmth and not enough competence may be likable but struggle to earn full trust. They often prioritize making others feel comfortable and avoid conflict at all costs, even to their own detriment.

Take Lisa, a middle school counselor. She was beloved by students and staff alike—always offering a kind word, remembering birthdays, and being the first to lend a helping hand. Her office was a haven where students felt heard and supported.

However, Lisa's overwhelming focus on being liked created its own set of challenges. When difficult situations arose—such as bullying or academic dishonesty—she struggled to have tough but necessary conversations. Her desire to avoid conflict led her to give vague advice rather than clear direction, leaving students uncertain about how to handle their problems.

When a student named Jamie was being cyberbullied, Lisa chose to focus on encouragement rather than direct action. Instead of confronting the bullies or involving their parents, as school policy required, she simply advised Jamie to *"stay positive"* and *"not let them get to you."* When Jamie's parents later discovered the extent of the bullying, they were furious that Lisa had failed to intervene effectively.

Her principal eventually called her in for a discussion. "Lisa, your heart is in the right place," he said, "but sometimes, being kind means being firm. These kids need clear boundaries and consequences, not just emotional support."

Lisa's case illustrates the dangers of prioritizing warmth at the expense of competence. While she was well-liked, people struggled to trust her in high-stakes situations. Her desire to please everyone ultimately left her ineffective when it mattered most.

The Path to Charisma

Understanding that charisma is the balance of warmth and competence is one thing—mastering that balance is another. The real question is: How do you display both warmth and competence in the right way?

This question is essential because it influences nearly every aspect of life:

- Your success in dating and romantic relationships
- How well you communicate with your children or get them to listen
- The way you present yourself at work and get noticed
- Your ability to be an effective leader or manager

Here's the good news: If you've been applying the principles in this book, you're growing your charisma. By showing warmth and competence—being empathetic and capable—you're becoming a more influential communicator.

The 3 C's: The Foundation of Charisma

Charisma naturally emerges when you master the balance of warmth and competence. The 3 C's—Curiosity, Clarity, and Courtesy—help you cultivate both in an authentic and effortless way.

Curiosity: The Bridge to Connection

When you lead with genuine curiosity, you:
- Demonstrate warmth by showing sincere interest in others.
- Display competence through thoughtful, insightful questions.
- Create space for meaningful, authentic conversations.
- Signal both genuine emotional intelligence and meaningful intellectual engagement.

Clarity: The Key to Trust

When you strive for clear understanding, you:

- Show competence through articulate, precise communication.
- Demonstrate warmth by seeking to understand others.
- Build trust through consistency and reliability.
- Foster psychological safety through transparency.

Courtesy: The Art of Social Intelligence

When you practice courtesy, you:

- Express warmth by treating others with respect and kindness.
- Exhibit competence by skillfully navigating social dynamics.
- Strengthen rapport through thoughtful, respectful behavior.
- Show emotional intelligence by choosing your words carefully to convey empathy and understanding.

Curiosity naturally signals warmth. When you follow it with clarity to deepen understanding, you demonstrate competence. And when you validate someone's thoughts, opinions, and emotions, you achieve both simultaneously. Finding this balance makes you more attractive to others and a more effective leader who inspires others to do more than the minimum and give their best.

Developing Your Charismatic Presence

The balanced display of warmth and competence isn't an inborn trait—it's a skill you can develop through practice. Here's how:

Building Warmth

- Practice active listening without interrupting.
- Show genuine interest in others' perspectives.
- Use engaging body language and facial expressions.
- Demonstrate empathy and understanding.
- Remember personal details and follow up on them.

Demonstrating Competence

- Follow through on commitments and promises.
- Speak with clarity and purpose.
- Maintain healthy boundaries without hesitation.
- Share knowledge generously and appropriately.
- Handle challenges with calm confidence.

Balancing Both

- Validate others' thoughts and experiences while offering practical solutions.
- Share personal stories highlighting strength and vulnerability.
- Give feedback that is both caring and constructive.
- Navigate tough conversations with empathy and directness.
- Lead by example while remaining warm, approachable, and relatable.

The Final Percent: Mastering Charisma

The 3 C's take you most of the way to maximizing your charisma. The final refinements come from fine-tuning how you present yourself and engage with others through:

- **Vocal tonality and pacing** – How you speak, including your tone and speed can make your message more engaging, clear, and impactful.
- **Body language and posture** – How you carry yourself signals confidence and presence.
- **Facial expressions** – Warmth and authenticity are reflected in your face.
- **Timing & delivery** – Knowing *when* to speak is as crucial as *what* you say.
- **Environmental awareness** – Charismatic individuals adjust seamlessly to different social settings.

The principles in this book will naturally help you develop these elements in any interaction. If you're interested in a deeper dive into these advanced techniques, I highly recommend *Cues:Master the Secret Language of Charismatic Communication* by Vanessa Van Edwards.

──────────── *KEY TAKEAWAYS* ────────────

Charisma isn't about becoming someone else—it's about refining the warmth and competence that already exist within you. As you integrate the 3 C's into your daily interactions, reflect on these questions:

- Am I expressing enough warmth in this situation?
- Am I demonstrating the right level of competence?
- How can I adjust my approach to balance both effectively?

By using **Curiosity, Clarity, and Courtesy,** you gain the fourth C—**Charisma**—the effortless charm that attracts people, builds trust, and boosts your influence.

True charisma isn't about being the loudest. It's about making real connections. You do this with a genuinely thoughtful and balanced presence. And the best part? This is a skill that anyone can develop with practice, awareness, and the right tools.

17

Mastering Vocal Tone:
The Hidden Key to Influence

"Y ou've got to record yourself," my mentor said just days before my microphone audition for a group fitness coaching position. "You need to hear what others hear."

I remember thinking, This will be easy. I've given hundreds of public talks. Then I played back my first recording. The voice I heard was flat, uninspiring—nothing like the energetic coach I imagined myself to be. That simple advice changed my audition and reshaped how I see communication.

What I learned in that moment was how essential the sound of my voice truly was in conveying energy, confidence, and enthusiasm. It wasn't just about what I said, but how I said it. Your voice is more than just sound—it's a powerful instrument that shapes how others perceive and respond to you. Similarly, your vocal tone isn't just an afterthought—it's a powerful tool that can either elevate or undermine your message. Like musical notes in a composition, different tones create different emotional responses in your listeners. Mastering the right tone ensures that your message lands exactly as you intend, creating a deeper connection.

There are three main vocal tonalities, each serving a specific purpose in communication:

1. **Supplicative** – A warm, inviting tone used to build rapport and connection.
2. **Neutral** – A balanced, even, and steady tone used for everyday communication to convey information.
3. **Authoritative** – A firm, commanding tone used for leadership and influence.

True communication mastery isn't about choosing one tone—it's about shifting between them at the right moments. Let's explore the supplicative tone—when to use it, when to avoid it, and how it shapes perceptions of status and influence.

Supplicative Tone: A Warm Invitation

Imagine walking into a tense room. A warm, gentle voice can instantly put people at ease. This is the supplicative tone. It helps build connection, demonstrates openness, and eases tension.

The supplicative tone conveys humility, friendliness, and gentleness. It's commonly used when asking questions, making requests, or extending a warm welcome. A well-placed supplicative tone can disarm hostility and encourage cooperation.

Think of a customer service representative calming an upset customer, or a teacher gently guiding a nervous student. Used strategically, this tone creates a sense of safety and approachability.

Using the supplicative tone too much or in the wrong situation can make you seem weak, unsure, or excessively needy. Most CEOs, government leaders, and managers don't often use this tone in speeches or directives. If a leader often sounds needy, people might interpret their words as requests rather than commands.

A clear example: Imagine a parent saying, "Please clean your room," in a soft, pleading tone. The child is likely to interpret it as a suggestion rather than an expectation. Compare that to a firm, confident tone: "It's time to clean your room now." The second statement conveys authority, making it far more effective.

A fun experiment: Observe a group conversation and listen for the supplicative tone. You'll quickly notice that the person with the highest status uses it the least, while the most validation-seeking person in the group uses it the most.

When to Use the Supplicative Tone

- ☑ When first greeting someone
- ☑ When asking a question
- ☑ To de-escalate tense situations
- ☑ To encourage openness or shift perspectives
- ☑ When expressing genuine excitement

When to Avoid the Supplicative Tone

- ☒ When giving directions or instructions
- ☒ When making important announcements
- ☒ When setting boundaries
- ☒ In leadership moments that require authority

This is the tone where "nice guys" and "people pleasers" often get stuck. If you've ever been labeled as *"too nice"* or struggled to be taken seriously in your professional or romantic relationships, your tone—not your personality—may be the issue.

The good news? You don't need to change who you are—just how you sound. Try adjusting your vocal tone, and you may find that people respect and respond to you in an entirely new way.

Next, let's explore the neutral tone—how it builds connection, when to use it, and how it fits into the rhythm of effective communication.

Neutral Tone: The Connection Builder

Think of the neutral tone as your conversational home base—steady, natural, and balanced. This is the tone you instinctively use with people you trust, whether it's your friend, partner, or a close colleague.

A neutral tone conveys equality. It doesn't defer (like the supplicative tone), nor does it assert dominance (like the authoritative tone). Instead, it creates a sense of psychological safety, where both parties feel comfortable expressing themselves freely.

As a recovering people-pleaser, I've found the neutral tone invaluable. It allows me to build genuine rapport without putting myself above or beneath others. If you struggle with being seen as "too nice," adjusting to a more neutral conversational tone can instantly shift how people perceive and respond to you.

How to Identify and Practice Neutral Tone

Try this experiment:

1. **Record yourself speaking in a supplicative tone**—notice how your sentences rise at the end, making statements sound like questions.
2. **Now, record yourself in a neutral tone**—keep a steady pitch throughout. End sentences level with the preceding words.
3. **Listen back**—which version sounds confident and natural?

This exercise is especially useful for public speaking or presentations. If you catch yourself using a supplicative tone, adjust to a more neutral, conversational tone to command greater respect and engagement.

When to Use the Neutral Tone

- ☑ In daily conversations
- ☑ When building rapport
- ☑ In team discussions
- ☑ During collaborative problem-solving
- ☑ When creating safe spaces for sharing

Benefits of the Neutral Tone

- Creates psychological safety
- Encourages open dialogue
- Builds lasting connections
- Maintains professional relationships
- Fosters trust and authenticity

A neutral tone isn't monotone—it should still be engaging! The key is modulation—varying pitch and pace while keeping your delivery natural and steady. This keeps conversations lively while maintaining an approachable and confident presence.

The Limitation of the Neutral Tone

While great for building trust, a neutral tone can sometimes be too passive. If you need to inspire action, shift to an authoritative tone.

Authoritative Tone: The Action Catalyst

The authoritative tone commands attention and drives action. It's direct, firm, and clear—not soft or gentle like the other two tones. Consider this example:

- *"Please clean your room?"* (Supplicative—sounds optional)
- *"Clean your room."* (Authoritative—non-negotiable)

The difference? The tone. The authoritative tone removes uncertainty. Leaders, parents, and law enforcement officers use this tone when they need immediate compliance.

A police officer saying, "License and registration." isn't making a polite request—it's a directive. The tone makes it clear.

When to Use the Authoritative Tone

☑ When urgency is required
☑ When requesting immediate action
☑ When conveying the seriousness of a situation

The Risk of Overuse

While the authoritative tone is powerful, overusing it can have unintended consequences. Used too frequently or in the wrong context can come across as harsh, demanding, or even dismissive. This can cause others to feel undervalued or defensive, potentially damaging relationships. For maxiumum effectiveness, use this tone strategically for moments that require urgency or authority. Balance it with curiosity and courtesy to foster connection and trust.

The Art of Tone-Shifting

True mastery isn't about using a single tone—it's about knowing when to shift between them.

A natural conversation follows a rhythm:

- **Opening/Greeting:** Supplicative (warm, welcoming)
- **Main Discussion:** Neutral (balanced, engaged)
- **Decision Points:** Authoritative (clear, directive)
- **Implementation/Next Steps:** Neutral or Collaborative
- **Closing:** Supplicative (friendly, encouraging)

For example, in a team meeting, a leader might:

- Start with a supplicative tone→"Good morning, everyone! Thanks for being here."
- Shift to neutral for discussion→"Let's talk about our current opportunities and challenges."
- Use authoritative for decisions→"Here's what we're going to do."
- Return to neutral for planning →"How can we execute the plan?"

My Experience with Tone-Shifting

Leading over 6,500 group fitness classes, I saw firsthand how tone affects engagement. Here's how I structured my vocal delivery:

- **Before class** – Supplicative (greeting members, creating a welcoming space)
- **During casual conversations** – Neutral (building rapport)
- **Starting class** – Authoritative (grabbing attention)
- **Giving instructions** – Authoritative (ensuring clarity)

I observed other coaches using supplicative or neutral tones when giving instructions. The result? Confusion and chaos. A lack of authority meant participants dismissed their guidance.

Using the right tone at the right moment made all the difference. You can apply this same flexibility to any leadership or communication setting.

Responding to Resistance

When you encounter pushback, use it as a cue to shift tones:

- **If your authoritative tone creates resistance**→Soften to a neutral, collaborative tone.
- **If your neutral tone isn't generating clarity**→Shift to an authoritative tone.
- **If engagement drops in neutral exchanges**→Add warmth with supplicative elements.

Resistance is often a signal that your tone needs adjusting. Becoming attuned to these moments makes your communication more adaptive, responsive, and effective.

Recording Exercise: Finding Your Voice

Here's a simple but powerful exercise to help you refine your vocal tones and practice smooth transitions between them:

Step 1: Record Yourself Using Different Tones
Say the following phrase in three distinct tones:
"We need to finish this project by Friday."
- Supplicative (soft, deferential)
- Neutral (balanced, conversational)
- Authoritative (firm, commanding)

Step 2: Listen for Key Differences
As you play back your recordings, pay attention to:
- Pitch Variations – Does your voice rise at the end (supplicative) or stay steady (neutral/authoritative)?
- Speed Changes – Do you slow down or speed up in certain tones?
- Emotional Impact – How does each version feel when you listen?
- Authenticity – Does any tone sound forced or unnatural?

Step 3: Practice Seamless Tone Transitions

Now, record yourself transitioning between tones:

- Supplicative→Neutral
- Neutral→Authoritative
- Authoritative→Neutral

Step 4: Reflect on Your Insights

- Did any tone feel awkward or unnatural?
- Does your authoritative tone sound too harsh or abrupt?
- Does your supplicative tone come across as weak rather than warm?
- Which tone feels most natural to you? Which one needs more work?

Many people discover they have a default tone—one they unconsciously use in most situations. Others find certain tones feel underdeveloped or difficult to express. The goal of this exercise is not just to master individual tones but to develop the ability to shift between them fluidly based on context.

Tone in Different Contexts

Mastering tone isn't about changing yourself. It's about expanding your range so you can communicate better in various situations. Here's how tone plays a role in different settings:

Professional Settings

- Meetings – Mostly neutral with shifts for clarity and emphasis.
- Presentations – A blend of neutral and authoritative to engage and lead.
- One-on-ones – Adapt based on the conversation's purpose (supportive vs. directive).

Personal Relationships

- Family Discussions – Mostly neutral, ensuring balance, calmness, and understanding.
- Conflict Resolution – Strategic tone shifting to de-escalate and find solutions.
- Intimate Conversations – Authentic neutral, fostering emotional connection.

Leadership Moments

- Vision Sharing – Authoritative, infused with inspiration and confidence.
- Team Building – Primarily neutral, creating trust, cooperation, and collaboration.
- Crisis Management – Clear authoritative tone to provide direction and communicate uregency.

Common Pitfalls to Avoid

Using only one tone too often can unintentionally send the wrong message. Here are three common tonal traps:

The People Pleaser (Stuck in Supplicative Mode)
- ☒ Undermines authority
- ☒ Signals low confidence
- ☒ Makes suggestions sound optional
- ☑ *Fix: Use a neutral or authoritative tone when clarity and direction are needed.*

The Constant Commander (Overuses Authoritative Tone)
- ☒ Creates resistance
- ☒ Can feel aggressive or unapproachable
- ☒ Damages trust in relationships
- ☑ *Fix: Balance with neutral or collaborative tones to build rapport.*

The Monotone Communicator (Lacks Tonal Variety)

☒ Sounds disengaged or robotic

☒ Misses emotional connection

☒ Reduces impact of key messages

☑ *Fix: Use modulation—vary pitch, pace, and emphasis—to keep your speech engaging.*

─────────────── *KEY TAKEAWAYS* ───────────────

Your voice is a strong tool for influence. It needs careful practice and strategic use. This chapter introduced three essential vocal tones—supplicative, neutral, and authoritative—each serving a distinct role in communication. True mastery isn't about sticking to one tone over the others. It's about being flexible and shifting tones based on your purpose, audience, and context.

Through the recording exercises, you may discover a default tone you rely on too often while others remain underdeveloped. Expanding your tonal range allows you to communicate more effectively without losing authenticity.

This week, challenge yourself to record three different conversations. Identify which tones you naturally default to and which feel uncomfortable. Focus on practicing transitions between tones that feel the most challenging. Your goal is to align your tone with both your authentic self and the intent of your message.

By mastering your vocal tone, you elevate your ability to connect, lead, and inspire—enhancing both your personal relationships and professional influence.

PART FIVE

Building Trust and Aligning Values

At the heart of every meaningful relationship is a deeper understanding of self. This section will guide you through discovering your core purpose, clarifying your personal values, and cultivating a refined approach to trust. You'll learn how your inner landscape influences your external connections and how to build relationships that not only endure but truly nourish your personal growth and potential.

18

Your Purpose, Values, and the Circle of Trust

T om McCallum once said, "We are not thinking beings who feel—we are emotional beings who think." This profound truth lies at the core of human connection. Relationships are built on communication—the way we express our thoughts, feelings, beliefs, and values to one another.

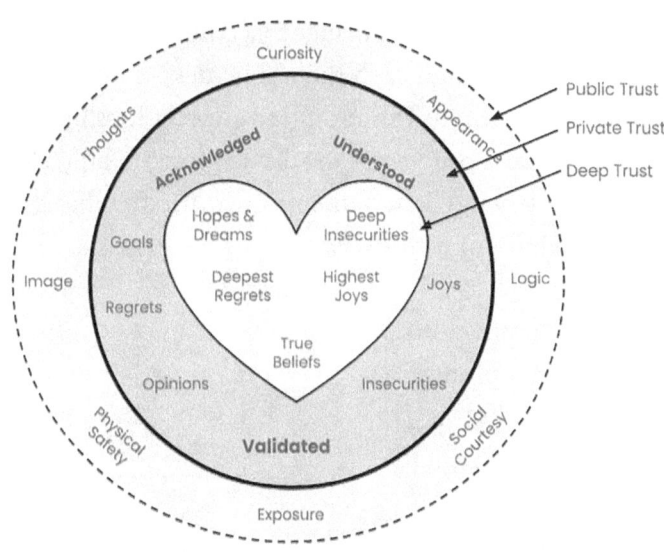

In this chapter, we explore the Circle of Trust framework, which visually illustrates how P.A.C.T.s (Purpose, Authenticity, Communication, and Trust) are formed. Understanding this framework will help you with three things:

1. Gain deeper insight into relationships.
2. Connect your emotions and thoughts.
3. Communicate who you really are at your core.

But first, let's begin a deeper exploration of the role purpose has in effective communication.

Understanding Your Purpose

Your strongest emotional reactions often point to your core values and purpose. In the Circle of Trust, the center is shaped like a heart to symbolize this connection. When our purpose and values match our audience's, we build trust and emotional safety. This helps us communicate openly and honestly. These are the happiest, most fulfilling relationships.

Communication acts as a bridge that connects your purpose and values to others that align with them. The deeper your connection to your intrinsic purpose, the stronger your relationships become.

Your purpose is your *why*—the driving force behind everything you do. It goes beyond achievements or goals; it's what gives your life meaning. Think of it this way:

Goals are destinations:
- Getting a promotion
- Buying a house
- Finding a partner

Purpose is your compass:
- What truly matters to you
- What gives your life meaning
- What you'd pursue even if no one noticed

Exercise: Finding Your Purpose

Take a moment to reflect on the following questions:

1. What activities make you lose track of time?
2. What problems do you love solving?
3. What topics make you light up when discussing them?
4. What would you do if money weren't a concern?

Your answers reveal key themes about your core purpose. Recognizing these patterns helps you see what drives you. This clarity helps you share your purpose more easily with others.

Defining Your Values

Your values guide your decisions and actions—they are the DNA of your personality, shaping who you are at your core. Living with purpose while staying true to your values leads to authenticity, which naturally strengthens your relationships.

Common values include:

- Integrity
- Growth
- Connection
- Creativity
- Service

Exercise: Identifying Your Values

Consider these questions:

1. What makes you proudest in life?
2. What angers you most about the world?
3. What do you admire most in others?
4. What would you stand up for, even if you were alone?

Once you identify and articulate your values, take a moment for self-evaluation:

- Do you live in alignment with your values regularly?
- How can you surround yourself with people who reflect these values?
- What actions can you take to reinforce the best aspects of your life?

For example, My best days come from helping others, working hard, and earning a good night's sleep. I also enjoy sharing good food, laughter, and special moments with people I admire. I strive to repeat these experiences as often as possible because they align with my values and purpose.

Bridging Purpose and Connection

Your strongest emotional reactions are often tied to your deepest values. This is why the heart sits at the center of the Circle of Trust—when our purpose and values align with those around us, we form deep, trusting connections.

However, many people struggle to create these bonds consistently. Why? We were never taught how to communicate in a way that fosters connection and trust. Some of us didn't grow up with positive role models for healthy communication, while others may have experienced relationships that lacked trust and understanding.

This book is not an exhaustive guide to solving every challenge in human connection. Instead, it is designed to help you understand universal principles of communication, connection, and trust, so you can apply them in your own unique way.

Now, let's dive deeper into The Circle of Trust and how it can transform your relationships.

The Circle of Trust Framework

Let's revisit the illustration. Think of your relationships like atoms forming bonds, with protective layers surrounding your core self. Each layer plays a crucial role in how we connect with others.

This illustration represents the layers of your authentic self. Authentic connection and trust emerge in the second layer *(private trust)*, while deep connection is achieved when you allow yourself to trust fully.

At the heart of it all, communication is the bridge that strengthens these bonds. The deeper and more meaningful the communication, the stronger the connection—reaching the innermost layers of trust and intimacy, just as the illustration depicts.

The Deep Trust Circle: Understanding Your Heart

Just as an atom's core holds its fundamental nature, your Deep Trust Circle contains everything that makes you uniquely you. This isn't just a metaphor—it's the control center of your emotional life, where your truest self resides. It's also the home of your purpose. When someone connects with this deeper layer of who you are, it creates a profound sense of alignment—one that reassures you that this relationship will support and enrich your life's purpose. This is a key pillar in forming your P.A.C.T.

At this core live the elements that define you:

- Your hopes and dreams
- Your deepest beliefs
- Your highest joys
- Your hidden fears
- Your guiding values

Let's take a close look at your heart with this illustration:

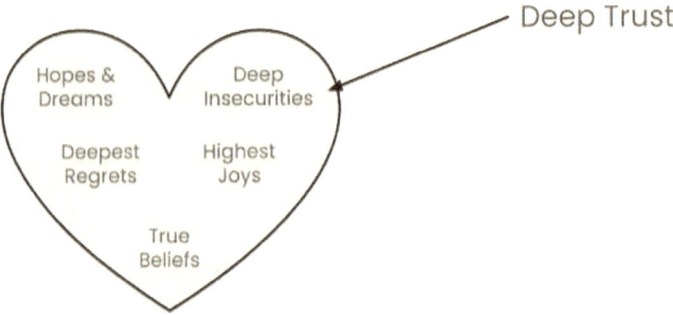

These aren't just characteristics; they are the forces that shape your decisions, relationships, and overall sense of fulfillment. They form your emotional compass, influencing every meaningful connection in your life.

How Your Emotional Compass Works

When something aligns with your core, you experience:

- ☑ Natural energy and motivation
- ☑ Deep, authentic connection
- ☑ Genuine excitement
- ☑ Effortless, flowing conversation
- ☑ A sense of being truly understood

When you connect with someone who shares your core values, the relationship feels natural and energizing.

When something conflicts with your core, you feel:

☒ An instant "ick" reaction
☒ Internal resistance
☒ Emotional discomfort
☒ A natural urge to withdraw

This explains why some relationships uplift you while others leave you drained. Think about the last time someone said something that felt instantly "off." That wasn't random discomfort—it was your emotional core sending you a message: "This doesn't align with who I truly am."

This internal warning system is crucial for navigating relationships and decisions that impact your well-being.

Understanding your Deep Trust Circle is crucial because:

1. It explains why certain relationships naturally flourish while others feel forced
2. It helps you recognize authentic connections versus superficial ones
3. It guides you toward relationships that energize rather than drain you

The key to creating meaningful connections lies in understanding not just our own Deep Trust Circle, but learning to recognize and respect it in others. Skillfully applying the 3 C's of communication is how you draw out and understand what lives in their Deep Trust Circle. When we communicate from this understanding, we can connect with the truest part of who someone is.

Reflection Exercise

Take a moment to identify:

- A relationship that naturally energizes you. What core values align?
- A situation that gives you that "ick" feeling. What core value is being challenged?
- A decision that felt "off." How does it conflict with your deepest beliefs?

The Private Trust Circle: Your Relationship Testing Ground

Because the people we allow into our inner world have the power to deeply affect us, The Deep Trust Circle is well protected by an outer layer, Private Trust, depicted here:

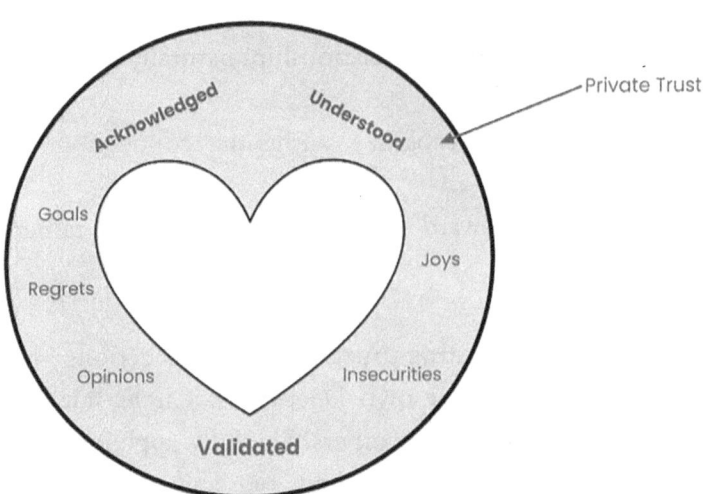

The Private Trust Circle acts as a protective barrier between our core self and the outside world. Think of this circle as your relationship laboratory—the space where you test potential deeper connections. It's not just about privacy; it's about emotional safety.

In this space, you selectively share:

- Personal stories that hold meaning
- Opinions you're still forming
- Carefully chosen vulnerabilities
- Goals and aspirations
- Moments of pride or embarrassment

This is where trust begins. Every time you share something personal, you're not just telling a story—you're testing the waters.

The Signals That Matter

When you share something meaningful, ask yourself:

- Does this person make me feel seen?
- Do they genuinely hear what I'm saying?
- Do they validate my experience?
- Can they hold space for my truth?

Think about the last time you shared something personal with someone. Their response either:

- Opened the door to deeper connection
- Confirmed the need to maintain distance

This isn't about being judgmental—it's about being intentional with your emotional energy.

Why This Process Matters

If someone responds with genuine understanding, you naturally open up more. If they dismiss or invalidate your experience, you instinctively pull back. This natural give-and-take protects your emotional core while allowing for meaningful connections where trust is earned.

The Private Trust Circle Works Both Ways

When others share with you, they're testing if you are safe for deeper connection. How you respond determines whether they move closer or keep their distance. This mutual trust-building process forms the foundation for authentic relationships. By understanding both your Deep and Private Trust Circles—and learning to navigate them wisely—you create relationships built on trust, respect, and genuine connection.

Practical Application: Moments That Build Trust

Notice how you feel when:

- A friend shares something personal
- A colleague confides in you
- Someone trusts you with their hopes or fears

Your response in these moments either builds or breaks trust. Recognizing this dynamic helps you:

- Create safer spaces for connection
- Recognize opportunities for deeper relationships
- Protect your emotional energy
- Build lasting trust

A Connection in Action: Sarah and Michael

A certain level of trust is necessary for maintaining even amicable working relationships or casual acquaintanceships.

Take Sarah and Michael, for example. During a team meeting, Sarah hesitated before voicing her concerns about a project's direction. Instead of dismissing her, Michael listened intently and asked thoughtful questions. That simple moment of respect transformed their working relationship. Sarah felt seen and understood, leading to more open communication. Over time, their mutual trust strengthened, benefiting the entire team.

This example illustrates the Private Trust Circle in action: one person takes a risk to share, and the other responds with understanding, deepening trust.

The Public Trust Circle

The Public Trust Circle is where we interact with the world from an emotionally safe distance.

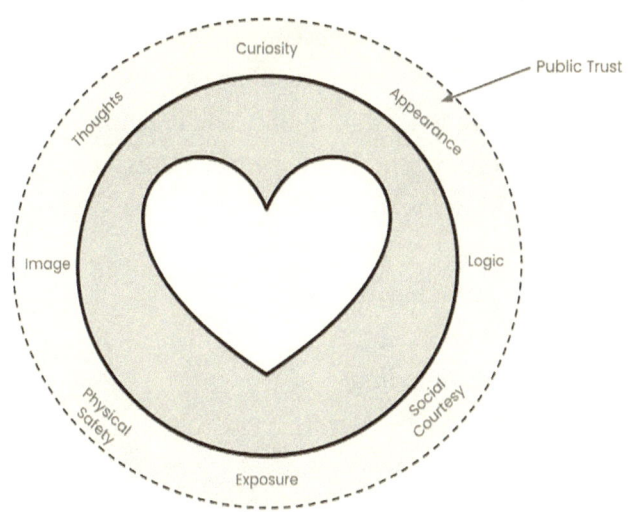

Think of it as your social interface—the version of yourself that you present in different environments. This outer layer helps you navigate social situations without compromising your true self.

Your Public Trust Circle adapts to various settings:

- Professional meetings
- First dates
- Social gatherings
- Casual interactions
- New relationships

In this circle, you:

- Present your professional image
- Navigate social settings
- Test initial connections
- Gauge relationship potential
- Maintain appropriate boundaries

For example, the version of yourself you present on a first date may be different from how you engage with a barista or how you present yourself in a job interview. This isn't about being fake—it's about being strategic with your energy and creating emotional safety.

This circle allows you to observe and assess your environment before deciding how much to reveal. In this space, you look for:

- Consistent behavior
- Mutual respect
- Basic understanding
- Social awareness
- Emotional safety

When things feel uncertain, we stick to our public self. When things feel safe, we naturally open up, allowing people deeper into our Circle of Trust.

A Connection in Motion: Alex and Maria

At a neighborhood barbecue, Alex observed Maria's interactions—she warmly greeted newcomers, respected personal space, and engaged in light conversation. When Maria asked about Alex's upcoming travels, he shared surface-level details about visiting Spain. Maria responded with interest but didn't probe too deeply, adding a brief comment about her own love of travel.

This casual exchange worked because both:

- Maintained appropriate social boundaries
- Showed basic courtesy and respect
- Engaged in light, contextually appropriate sharing
- Responded with social awareness
- Recognized the public nature of the setting

This demonstrates how the Public Trust Circle functions—low-risk interactions test compatibility before any deeper connection develops.

Chemistry and Trust:
The Atomic Structure of Relationships

The Public, Private, and Deep Trust Circles work together like the structure of an atom. We are layered and complex, yet our connections can be understood and nurtured in a structured way.

With the right chemistry, we form strong bonds—relationships that enhance our productivity, happiness, and emotional stability.

P.A.C.T. = Circles of Trust Bonding

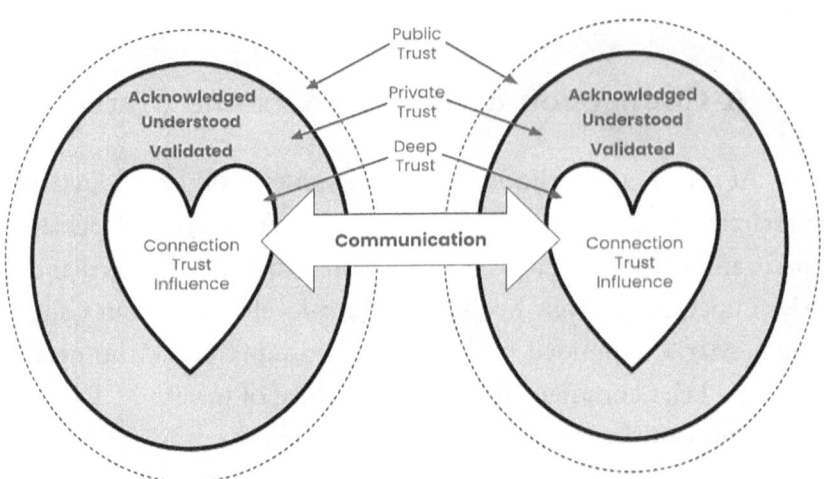

Communication is the key to building the chemistry that connects us with others (as shown in the illustration above). As discussed, it falls into two categories: toxic or attractive.

- Toxic communication creates distance, pushing people away and making genuine connection difficult—if not impossible. It often leads to misunderstandings, frustration, and emotional disconnection.
- Attractive communication, on the other hand, fosters trust, understanding, and meaningful relationships.

Many people unknowingly engage in toxic communication, unaware of its impact on their relationships. Recognizing these patterns is the first step toward cultivating healthier connections.

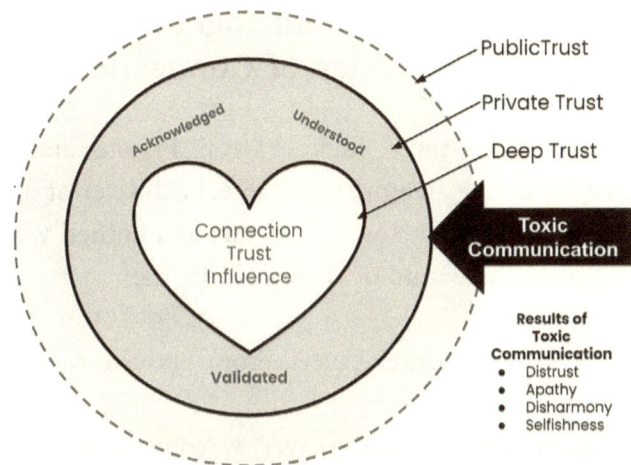

This illustration highlights how Toxic Communication (right arrow) acts as a barrier, preventing access to deeper levels of Private and Public Trust in others. Attractive Communication has the opposite effect—it strengthens connections, fostering trust and emotional safety.

Attractive Communication bridges the gap between individuals, enhancing all aspects of happy, successful, and fulfilling relationships.

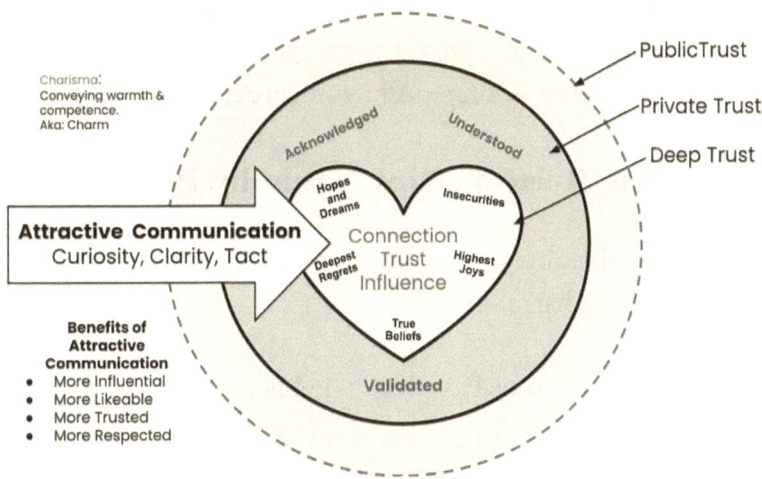

This illustration demonstrates how Attractive Communication (left arrow) opens the path to deeper levels of trust, allowing for more meaningful and authentic connections.

Bringing It All Together:
The Chemistry of Connection

Think of these three circles—Deep, Private, and Public—working together like an atom's structure. Each layer of trust serves a distinct purpose, but they work together as a unified whole.

The Atomic Structure of Trust includes the:

- Public Trust (Outer Layer) – Your outward social interface with the world
- Private Trust (Middle Layer) – Your testing ground for deeper connections
- Deep Trust (Core) – Your emotional center and truest self

When all three circles function properly:

- Public Trust (Outer Layer) – Establishes a sense of safety and shared compatibility
- Private Trust (Middle Layer) – Tests the potential for deeper connection
- Deep Trust (Core) – Allows for true, authentic bonding

How Relationships Naturally Progress

Like in chemistry, relationships naturally progress when these layers interact in harmony.

1. Start with social courtesy (Public) – Light conversation, respectful boundaries
2. Move to careful sharing (Private) – Testing emotional safety
3. Develop genuine connection (Deep) – Trust and authenticity

Exercise: Trust Mapping

Draw Your Own Circle of Trust:

1. List what belongs in each circle. What parts of yourself do you share at each level?
2. Identify who has access to each layer. Who do you trust at each level?
3. Recognize where boundaries need strengthening. Where do you need more protection?
4. Plan conscious sharing strategies. How can you communicate in a way that builds trust?

——————————— *KEY TAKEAWAYS* ———————————

Understanding your purpose, values, and trust circles empowers you to:

- Create authentic connections
- Protect your emotional energy
- Build lasting relationships
- Navigate social situations wisely

Just as an atom needs all its layers to function, you need all of your trust circles to create healthy relationships. Trust builds naturally when we respect these layers and communicate in a way that fosters genuine connection.

Additionally, understanding the impact of Toxic vs. Attractive Communication helps explain why some relationships thrive while others struggle. As depicted in the illustration below, Attractive Communication fosters trust, influence, likability, and respect—ultimately strengthening connection. In contrast, Toxic Communication breeds distrust, apathy, disharmony, and selfishness, creating barriers that hinder deeper relationships.

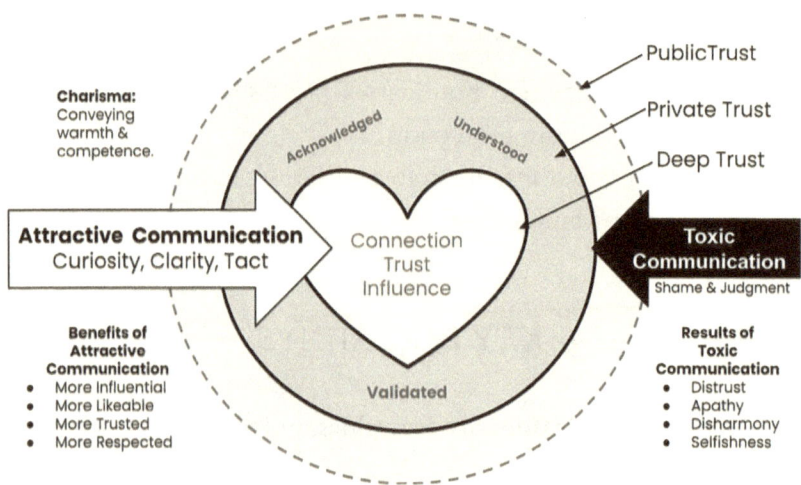

In the next chapter, we'll explore how to use this understanding to break free from past patterns that might be blocking you from creating the relationships you deserve.

19

Breaking Free from The Past

What you think about your past shapes your future and how you communicate. Read that again carefully. Notice what I didn't say—I *didn't* say, *your past shapes your future*. Instead, it's your interpretation of your past that determines your future.

This distinction is critical. While you *can't* change past events, you *can* change how you carry and interpret them. This isn't just positive thinking—it's grounded in science. Research on neuroplasticity proves that the brain can form new neural pathways throughout life, allowing us to reshape our beliefs and behaviors.

How Interpretation Shapes Experience

Consider two individuals who experience the same childhood difficulty—say, their parents divorcing. One grows up carrying fear and distrust into relationships, while the other develops deep empathy and strong communication skills. The event was the same, but their interpretation determined the trajectory of their lives.

The Science of Energy and Connection

Have you ever walked into a room and felt the energy shift? Or met someone whose presence instantly put you at ease—or, conversely, made you uncomfortable? Have you ever heard or said, "You have great energy" or "I love your vibe"?

Dr. James Oschman, a pioneer in energy medicine, has documented how electromagnetic fields influence everything from cellular function to interpersonal connections. Here's what's fascinating—humans generate an electromagnetic field around them. This isn't mystical thinking; it's measurable science.

Your nervous system produces this field, and its quality is shaped by two primary factors:

1. **Your thoughts** – The internal dialogue and beliefs you hold
2. **Your emotions** – Your conscious and unconscious emotional states you experience

This explains why some people radiate confidence and warmth, while others seem to drain the energy from a room. If our thoughts and emotions dictate our energetic presence, then mastering them allows us to control our vibe—which in turn affects every interaction and relationship in our lives.

The Battle in Your Brain

Understanding this is powerful—but controlling thoughts and emotions isn't always easy. Why? Because past experiences shape subconscious beliefs, which influence our reactions, often without us realizing it.

Take Caroline's story:

The coffee shop buzzed with morning activity as Caroline stared at the empty chair across from her. Her date was fifteen minutes late—again. A familiar voice whispered in her head: They always leave. Her chest tightened. Memories of childhood abandonment resurfaced. The smell of coffee and quiet chatter faded as old wounds threatened to overwhelm her present moment.

But Caroline had done the work. She took a deep breath and consciously reframed her thought: This says more about his time management than my worth. I deserve someone who respects my time, and I can choose how I respond. The tightness in her chest eased. She sat up straighter, reclaiming her power.

This moment illustrates a universal struggle: the conflict between conscious desires and subconscious programming. Our brains store emotional experiences as memories. These memories shape our beliefs. These beliefs quietly influence how we communicate, connect, and make decisions.

The Subconscious Scripts Running Your Life

Your brain is incredibly efficient at transforming experiences into belief systems. Consider how holiday experiences—whether joyful or painful—can shape someone's emotional responses for decades.

Our memories shape our expectations. Our expectations shape our reality. But the good news is that you can rewrite the script. By recognizing outdated beliefs and actively reshaping them, you can break free from the past and communicate with more confidence, clarity, and connection.

The Subconscious Joy Script

For Maria, Christmas is a season of warmth and connection. The scent of cinnamon and pine triggers cherished memories— family gatherings filled with laughter, the soft hum of holiday music, and flour-dusted aprons as she and her grandmother baked cookies together. She recalls her father reading stories by the fireplace while her mother lovingly arranged presents under the tree.

Her brain stored these positive experiences as a "safety" signal, reinforcing an emotional association between the holidays and feelings of love and belonging. Decades later, the first notes of a Christmas carol can still lift her mood, opening her heart to new connections. Because of these subconscious patterns, she naturally seeks out and fosters joyful relationships, especially during the holiday season.

The Subconscious Pain Script

For James, holiday music evokes an entirely different set of memories—arguments over money, empty chairs at dinner, and the shame of explaining to friends why Santa didn't bring more presents. He remembers the tension in his mother's voice as she explained, once again, why his father wouldn't be coming home for Christmas. Storefront holiday displays only heightened the ache of comparison, making his stomach twist with silent resentment.

His brain stored these experiences as threats, triggering a subconscious withdrawal response whenever the holidays approached. Now, as an adult, he avoids gatherings without fully understanding why, unconsciously shielding himself from expected disappointment. Unfortunately, this self-protective pattern reinforces isolation, making meaningful connection even harder to sustain.

These contrasting scripts illustrate why controlling our thoughts and emotions isn't just a matter of willpower. When strong emotions are tied to specific experiences—or reinforced over time—they become deeply wired into our subconscious. No amount of positive affirmations alone can override what has been hardwired into our brain's emotional circuitry.

If you've experienced deep emotional trauma or abuse, rewiring these subconscious patterns is even more challenging—but not impossible. Healing begins with awareness and intentional effort.

Understanding Trauma's Impact

Emotional wounds can hurt more than people think. They can come from fear, sadness, shame, guilt, anger, neglect, betrayal, grief, or injustice. Trauma generally falls into two categories, each affecting how we form relationships and communicate:

Big 'T' Trauma – The Earthquakes

These are **single, significant events** that shake our emotional foundation and shape how we approach trust and connection:

- Betrayal by trusted figures
- Sudden loss of a loved one (grief)
- Physical or emotional violations
- Major life disruptions
- Catastrophic events or accidents
- Severe neglect or abandonment

These events often lead to deep-seated fears, shaping our ability to trust others and communicate openly.

Little 't' Trauma – The Constant Drips

These are **repeated, smaller experiences** that gradually erode emotional resilience over time:

- Consistent criticism
- Emotional neglect
- Subtle undermining
- Chronic disappointment
- Regular dismissal of feelings
- Persistent lack of validation
- Microaggressions
- Ongoing instability

These experiences may seem small on their own, but their impact adds up over time. They change how we view relationship and rewire our self-worth, communication styles, and emotional openness.

How Trauma Shapes P.A.C.T.

Sustained emotional trauma and abuse affect each pillar of P.A.C.T., influencing how we connect with ourselves and others:

- **Purpose** – Trauma distorts self-worth, making it difficult to identify or believe in your purpose. Instead of pursuing what fulfills you, you may prioritize pleasing others to fill an emotional void.
- **Authenticity** – You unconsciously attract the familiar, even if it doesn't align with your best interests. This often leads to repeating painful relationship patterns.
- **Communication** – Expressing your true self becomes difficult, making meaningful connections feel out of reach.
- **Trust** – Fear of abandonment, rejection, or failure makes trust in relationships challenging. The subconscious belief that history will repeat itself keeps you guarded.

Recognizing these patterns is the first step toward breaking free from them. Healing is possible, but it requires intentional effort to rewire the subconscious mind and reclaim control over how we connect, communicate, and experience relationships.

The Journey of Healing from Emotional Trauma

I'll share with you some deeply personal experiences. I trust they will be received with understanding and compassion, as I believe they can illuminate how emotional trauma and abuse shape us.

Here are some of the Big T emotional traumas in my life:

- Molested by a family member at 7 years old.
- My father abandoned me at 9 years old.
- My mother died when I was 14.
- My grandmother died when I was 18.
- My aunt and uncle stole my inheritance, which could have funded my college education or home purchase.

Alongside these major traumatic events, I also survived a great deal of emotional abuse:

- My aunt and uncle, who became my legal guardians after my mother's death, consistently shamed and guilted me.
- I was bullied in school for my race.
- I endured a marriage filled with gaslighting, shame, guilt, and betrayal.

I won't go into further detail about each of these situations because I imagine you understand the pain, and perhaps even relate to some of these experiences.

These events could have easily defined my future relationships, and initially, they did. Like many trauma survivors, I found myself:

- Attracting people who reinforced familiar pain patterns
- Creating overly rigid boundaries that prevented genuine connection and emotional openness
- Sabotaging potentially healthy relationships
- Accepting less than I deserved due to the fear of being rejected and alone
- Struggling to maintain long-term relationships
- Distrusting genuine care and support from others

I share these personal things not to gain pity or praise, but to show that if you've endured emotional trauma or abuse, you can break free from its grip. I am not alone in this, and neither are you.

How Trauma Impacts Relationships and Communication

So, how do these emotionally traumatic and abusive events affect how someone interacts and communicates in their relationships? Most often, instead of attracting emotionally healthy people, individuals with unhealed wounds attract others who are similarly wounded. We unconsciously draw in what feels familiar—often, pain and dysfunction. And that's how these patterns are reinforced.

A key sign of someone with unhealed emotional wounds is their tendency to seek love or approval from people who are emotionally difficult, unreliable, or even abusive. Without healing, the subconscious mind will continue to seek out these familiar dynamics, unknowingly reinforcing the cycle.

The Battle Between the Mind and the Heart

When we don't heal our emotional wounds, our brain and emotions battle. Spoiler alert: the subconscious brain always wins.

Your logical, conscious brain may say:

"I don't want to repeat this. I deserve better. Let's find something better. Let's be better."

But your subconscious brain responds with:

"We will never forget what happened to us. I will protect you by reminding you of the danger whenever I sense it."

And then your figurative heart joins in:

"I agree with the conscious brain. But I also don't want to be alone. I don't want to be hurt again. What if I never find someone who understands me like this person does?"

This tug-of-war creates attachment issues, where your thoughts and emotions send out conflicting signals. When what's familiar to you is the emotional pattern tied to trauma and abuse, you'll continue to attract relationships that resonate with that energy.

Because the heart can become desperate for connection, you may avoid setting healthy boundaries or walking away from relationships—even when the red flags are obvious. Alternatively, you might build walls so high that no one can meet your unrealistic standards. Then, when they inevitably fail, you may think, "There are no good ones out there," or worse, "I'm not good enough."

Breaking Free from the Pattern

How do you break free from this pattern? The solution is simple in theory, but it requires consistent practice and effort:

- Change your thoughts
- Change your emotions
- Change your vibe

However, implementing these changes requires understanding how your thoughts, emotions, and body connect, as well as creating new patterns. When you reframe your past life events in your subconscious and replace old beliefs with more empowering ones, you'll begin to attract new experiences and relationships.

Is Therapy Worth It?

Therapy has become more popular and accepted in recent years. It's no longer something people shy away from or stigmatize. Therapy helps you understand your emotions, validate them, and trace their origins. But, in my experience, therapy alone wasn't always enough to reframe my traumatic memories or effectively regulate my emotions.

185

Others I've spoken with have shared similar experiences—some found therapy transformative, while others felt it fell short. This varied experience is why some say "therapy is worth it!" while others are hesitant.

So, is therapy worth it for you?

The effectiveness of therapy depends on several factors:

- A strong rapport with your therapist
- Sessions that help you understand and reframe your past life events and beliefs
- Practical strategies to regulate your emotions

For me, combining therapy with nervous system regulation techniques was what truly produced powerful results.

The Body-Mind Connection

Here's a fascinating insight: While memories live in your brain, emotions reside in your body.

Think about it:

- Where do you feel joy? (Often in the chest and face)
- Where do you feel anxiety and stress? (Usually in the stomach or throat)
- Where do you feel confidence? (Typically in your posture and shoulders)
- Where do you feel peace? (In the breath and muscles)
- Where does excitement bubble up? (In the chest and limbs)
- Where does fear freeze you? (In the gut and spine)
- Where do you feel lust? (Below the heart)

Recognizing where these emotions reside in your body can help you quickly identify them and regain control. The faster you can recognize and label your emotions, the quicker your brain can process them and shift your focus.

The Power of Self-Regulation

When you know where your emotions reside in your body, you can regulate them by consciously shifting your focus. For example, if I feel anxiety in my chest, I can breathe deeply and shift my focus to calm the area, helping my body relax. By combining this with reframing memories to bring out positive emotions, you can build self-regulation skills. Many people don't even realize this is possible.

This is far more than just repeating positive affirmations. It's about practicing a real skill that enables you to shift your thoughts and emotions on demand. Once you master this, you can reframe any situation or memory into something that helps you, rather than feeling like a victim of your past.

My Personal Journey

I learned how to regulate my emotions through therapy and deep self-awareness. I used to tense up and feel anxious whenever I explored my curiosity. The lingering emotional residue from past experiences—like being punished for my curiosity—made me believe I was bad, selfish, or would inevitably disappoint others. But through consistent therapy and intentional healing work, I learned to recognize these emotional triggers, reframe the painful memories, and replace the feelings of shame with ones of joy, appreciation, and deep self-compassion.

It's not about forcing emotions or ignoring unpleasant feelings. It's about recognizing what you're feeling, understanding its impact on your body, and choosing to shift it into something that better serves you. This super skill allows you to take control of your energy and emotions at any moment, creating new neural pathways and building emotional resilience.

Once you master this skill, you'll be better equipped to understand your circle of trust and apply the P.A.C.T. principles for healthier, more fulfilling relationships.

Practical Applications

Now, let's explore how to apply these concepts in different real-world scenarios:

The Professional Setting

Lisa had a deep-seated fear of team presentations after being humiliated by a former boss. Each time she had to present, she used the following strategies:

- Acknowledge the tension in her shoulders, recognizing the physical signs of anxiety.
- Remind herself that this response was tied to old programming, not her current reality.
- Focus on her current expertise and the value she brought to the team.
- Ground herself in the present by seeking support from her colleagues or focusing on a positive aspect of her current work environment.
- Visualize herself executing a successful presentation and the positive emotions that would follow.
- After the presentation, she would acknowledge and internalize where in her body she felt a sense of success and pride.

In a Dating Context

Marcus struggled with trust after experiencing betrayals in past relationships. When meeting someone new, he made a conscious effort to:

- Notice his instinct to withdraw when he felt vulnerable or uncertain.
- Identify where fear sat in his body, whether it was in his chest, stomach, or throat.
- Choose curiosity over protection, opening himself up to the present moment instead of assuming the worst.
- Stay present by relying on the evidence of the current situation, rather than projecting past patterns.
- Share vulnerability slowly, allowing trust to build over time.
- Honor his boundaries while remaining open to connection.

Within Family Dynamics

Elena felt triggered by family gatherings, particularly during the holidays. To manage, she developed a strategy that included:

- Preparing emotionally beforehand by acknowledging her feelings and setting intentions for the event.
- Setting clear boundaries about how much time she would spend at gatherings and the types of interactions she was comfortable with.
- Creating new traditions that fostered positive emotions and allowed her to feel in control.
- Focusing on building positive associations with family time, such as highlighting joyful moments.
- Planning strategic exits when she felt overwhelmed or needed a break.
- Cultivating supportive connections by nurturing relationships with family members who respected her boundaries and supported her emotional well-being.

Tools for Transformation

Here are practical tools to help you improve your body awareness and emotional regulation:

1. Body Awareness Practice

- Start your day with a body scan to check in with how you're feeling physically and emotionally.
- Notice where emotions settle in your body and track any recurring patterns.
- Track the connection between your thoughts and physical sensations to uncover insights into your emotional triggers.
- Practice shifting your state intentionally by using deep breathing, visualization, or grounding techniques.
- Document your discoveries in a journal and build a personal emotional map to understand how your body responds to different emotions.

2. Thought Reframing

- Question automatic negative thoughts and challenge them by looking for evidence that contradicts those beliefs.
- Create empowering alternate interpretations to replace limiting ones, focusing on growth rather than protection.
- Celebrate small victories and progress as you rewire your thought patterns.
- Over time, this practice will build new neural pathways that support a more positive mindset.

3. Energy Management

- Recognize your typical energy patterns by noting what raises or lowers your vibration.
- Notice how your environment and relationships influence your energy.

- Create environments that support a positive and high-vibration state, such as decluttering your space or engaging in activities that make you feel grounded.
- Choose relationships that enhance your frequency and protect your emotional space from draining influences.
- Cultivate uplifting activities like meditation, exercise, or hobbies that rejuvenate your energy.

4. Boundary Setting

- Identify your non-negotiables, the things you need to feel safe and respected in relationships.
- Communicate your limits clearly and assertively, without guilt or hesitation.
- Honor your needs to avoid burnout or resentment.
- Adjust your boundaries as you grow and evolve, recognizing that they may need to shift based on new circumstances or personal growth.
- Practice saying no without guilt and celebrate the strength it takes to protect your energy and well-being.

KEY TAKEAWAYS

Breaking free from your past is not about denying or suppressing your history; it's about:

- Understanding how past experiences shaped you and recognizing patterns that no longer serve you.
- Creating new neural pathways through conscious choices that allow you to shift old narratives.
- Building relationships that support your growth by practicing self-awareness, emotional regulation, and healthy boundaries.

- Honoring your journey while embracing the changes that will bring you closer to your best self.
- Celebrating your resilience and the progress you've made along the way.

Your past experiences may have shaped your initial programming, but your present choices will shape your future connections. As you move forward with the P.A.C.T. principles, understanding how your thoughts and emotions influence your relationships will empower you to create more fulfilling, supportive connections.

In the next chapter, we'll dive deeper into how this foundation of self-awareness enhances your ability to form meaningful connections through P.A.C.T., building on the emotional intelligence and self-regulation skills we've just explored.

20

Creating Healthy Boundaries: Protecting Your Circle of Trust

Maya sat in her therapist's office, tears streaming down her face. "I don't understand," she said, clutching a tissue. "I keep trying to be understanding, supportive, and there for everyone. But I feel so… empty—like I'm constantly giving pieces of myself away, and there's nothing left."

Her therapist leaned forward slightly. "Maya, when was the last time you said 'no' to someone who needed your help?"

Maya fell silent. The weight of her unspoken answer hung in the room. A flicker of realization passed over her face—a quiet acknowledgment of a pattern she hadn't named until now.

This scene plays out in various forms every day—especially for those who are highly empathetic or have experienced emotional abuse or trauma. These individuals often find it difficult to set boundaries. They mistake boundaries for selfishness or unkindness, but nothing could be further from the truth.

Healthy boundaries are not walls; they're bridges to more honest, sustainable relationships. They allow us to give from a place of wholeness rather than depletion.

Understanding Boundaries
Through the Circle of Trust

Remember the concept of the Circle of Trust? The concentric circles—Deep Trust, Private Trust, and Public Trust—are not just about understanding relationships; they also provide an excellent framework for establishing healthy boundaries.

Imagine your Circle of Trust as a beautiful garden:

- The **Deep Trust circle** is where your most cherished plants reside, requiring the most careful protection.
- The **Private Trust circle** is like your garden fence, controlling access to your inner sanctum.
- The **Public Trust circle** is your front yard—visible to all but still part of your property.

Just as a garden needs both nurturing and protection, your relationships need connection and boundaries.

The P.A.C.T. Approach to Boundaries

Let's explore how the P.A.C.T. method can help us create and maintain healthy boundaries. Boundaries should reflect and protect your core purpose and values. Consider Diana's story:

Diana loved her job as a graphic designer but was constantly bombarded with after-hours client requests. Her core purpose was clear: to create beautiful, impactful designs. However, late-night requests were draining her creativity and impacting her work quality. After much reflection, she set a firm boundary: no client calls after 6 PM unless previously scheduled.

At first, she was concerned it might seem unprofessional. But by clearly communicating her boundaries and offering alternative solutions, such as early morning calls or scheduled evening sessions, she gained more respect from her clients. Her boundaries protected her purpose while still serving others effectively.

Authenticity in Boundaries

Strong boundaries, when communicated clearly and authentically, actually make you more attractive—not less. They demonstrate:

- Self-respect
- Clear values
- Emotional maturity
- Reliable behavior

Take James, for example, who struggled with a friend who constantly borrowed money. Instead of avoiding his friend or harboring resentment, James had a clear conversation:

"I value our friendship deeply, which is why I need to be honest. I can't continue lending money because it's affecting our relationship. I'd be happy to help you explore budgeting strategies if you'd like."

This conversation didn't weaken their friendship; it strengthened it by addressing the underlying issue. It replaced a pattern of financial enablement with genuine support.

Communicating Boundaries Effectively

The key to effective boundary-setting is the 3 C's:

1. Curiosity
- Understand your own needs
- Explore others' perspectives
- Seek win-win solutions

2. Clarity
- Be specific about your limits
- Express boundaries directly
- Explain why when appropriate

3. Courtesy
- Communicate with respect
- Acknowledge others' feelings
- Offer alternative solutions when possible

Here's an example of effective boundary communication:

"I notice our conversations often extend late into the night (Curiosity). While I deeply value our talks, I need to end phone calls by 10 PM to maintain my sleep schedule (Clarity). I'd love to find another time when we can talk without feeling rushed (Courtesy)."

This approach—combining warmth with clarity—ensures that your boundaries are respected while minimizing the chance of offense.

Trust Through Boundaries

Strong boundaries build trust, not undermine it. They create:

- Predictability in relationships
- Mutual respect
- Clear expectations
- Emotional safety

Common Boundary Challenges

The People-Pleaser's Dilemma
Like Maya in the opening story, many people struggle with setting boundaries out of fear of disappointing others. It's important

to remember: boundaries aren't walls—they're bridges to stronger, healthier relationships.

The Guilt Trip

Sometimes, people will try to make you feel guilty for setting boundaries. This might sound like:

- "But we've always done it this way..."
- "If you cared, you'd help..."
- "I guess I just care more about our relationship..."

These are manipulation tactics, not valid reasons to abandon your boundaries. When faced with these types of statements, it's important to recognize them as signals that the relationship might need re-evaluation.

The Boundary Pusher

Some people will repeatedly test and push your boundaries. This requires consistent reinforcement and, in some cases, stronger boundaries. If someone constantly challenges your boundaries instead of respecting them, this may be a sign that you need to reconsider your relationship with that person or organization.

Creating Healthy Boundaries: A Practical Guide

Now that we understand the importance of boundaries in fostering healthy relationships, the next step is learning how to establish boundaries that strengthen these connections. Here are four key considerations for setting healthy boundaries in your relationships:

1. Identify Your Circles

Start by defining your circles of trust:

- **Deep Trust:** What requires your strongest protection?
- **Private Trust:** What needs careful sharing and who do you trust with this?
- **Public Trust:** What are you comfortable sharing widely with others?

Understanding which aspects of your life belong in each circle helps you know where to set limits and how to protect your emotional well-being.

2. Align With Your Purpose

Your boundaries should align with your core values and goals. Ask yourself:

- Do your boundaries protect what matters most to you?
- Are your relationships supporting your purpose?
- Where do you need stronger boundaries to better protect your time, energy, and values?

When boundaries reflect your deeper purpose, they become a powerful tool to reinforce your vision for the future, making it easier to say no when necessary and stay aligned with what truly matters.

3. Communicate Effectively

Clear and compassionate communication is key when setting boundaries. Use the following formula to guide your conversations with others:

- **Start with:** "I notice..." (State the behavior or situation you've observed)
- **Follow with:** "I need..." (Specify your boundary)
- **End with:** "Would you be willing..." (Make a request for how you'd like things to change)

For example, "I notice that I'm often asked to work late on projects (observation). I need to have my evenings free to recharge (boundary). Would you be willing to schedule meetings earlier in the day? (request)"

4. Maintain Consistency

Setting boundaries is only effective if they're communicated and enforced consistently.

- **Enforce them respectfully:** Be firm but kind when reminding others of your limits.
- **Address violations promptly:** When someone oversteps your boundary, address it right away.
- **Adjust as needed:** Boundaries may evolve as you grow, so be flexible and adjust them when appropriate.

Signs Your Boundaries Need Strengthening

If you're noticing any of these warning signs, it might be time to reassess and strengthen your boundaries:

- Feeling resentful in relationships
- Constantly feeling drained or depleted of energy
- Difficulty saying no
- Feeling taken for granted
- Compromising your values
- Experiencing chronic stress or anxiety
- Avoiding difficult conversations to keep the peace

The Power of No

Learning to say no is key to establishing healthy boundaries. Here are some ways to say it gracefully:

1. The Simple No
"No, I won't be able to take that on."

2. The Appreciative No
"I'm honored you thought of me, but I need to decline."

3. The Alternative No
"I can't do that, but here's what I can offer..."

4. The Clear No
"This doesn't align with my current priorities, so I need to say no."

By practicing these different types of "no," you can maintain your boundaries with respect and clarity, without feeling guilty.

Boundaries in Action: A Case Study

Let's revisit Maya's story from earlier. After recognizing her boundary struggles with her therapist, Maya took small steps to protect her time and energy.

First, she began by protecting her lunch break at work—no more working through lunch to help colleagues. At first, she felt guilty, but soon she noticed a significant shift: her afternoon productivity improved, her stress levels decreased, and her colleagues respected her more.

Encouraged by this success, she expanded her boundaries:

- She set specific visiting hours for family members.
- She declined non-essential social obligations.
- She made sure to protect her morning routine.

Within months, Maya reported feeling more energized, respected, and connected in her relationships. Her boundaries didn't push people away—they created space for healthier, more fulfilling connections.

———— *KEY TAKEAWAYS* ————

Remember:

- Boundaries protect relationships, they don't damage them.
- Clear boundaries attract healthy connections.
- Consistent boundaries build trust.
- Strong boundaries enable deeper intimacy.

As you apply the Circle of Trust and P.A.C.T. principles to your boundaries, start small. Choose one area where you need stronger boundaries and begin there. Watch how protecting your energy helps you create more meaningful and supportive relationships.

Your boundaries are not walls that isolate you. Rather, they provide the foundation for lasting, respectful relationships while allowing you to honor your well-being. Boundaries are essential for maintaining strong P.A.C.T.s across all aspects of your life.

In the next chapter, we'll explore how to navigate difficult relationships, specifically how to handle narcissistic behavior while maintaining your emotional health.

21

How to Communicate
with a Narcissist

I rene sat across from me during our coaching session, tears streaming down her face. "I feel like I'm going crazy," she said, clutching a tissue. "One moment, he's the most charming, supportive person in the world. The next, I'm walking on eggshells, terrified that anything I say will trigger an explosion. Am I the problem?"

Irene's story mirrors so many others I've heard—and even my own experiences. After two marriages spanning twelve years with partners who seemed to prioritized their own egos over mutual growth, I understand the confusion, self-doubt, and emotional exhaustion of dealing with narcissistic behavior.

What Does It Mean to Be a Narcissist?

The term "narcissist" has become common in everyday conversation, yet most people have different ideas about what it truly means. You may know someone whom you believe is a narcissist—perhaps a past partner, a family member, or even a colleague. However, defining narcissism is tricky. According to

Dr. Ramani, a renowned psychologist, most narcissists remain undiagnosed because they are unlikely to seek therapy or face their issues directly. Despite this, many of us have had personal or professional encounters with people exhibiting narcissistic traits.

It's essential to grasp what narcissism truly entails, as many people will inevitably cross paths with someone who demonstrates narcissistic behavior, whether in the workplace, in social settings, or within personal relationships. If you're not careful, you could find yourself subjected to emotional abuse. However, by understanding how to identify narcissism, you can protect yourself and learn how to coexist with narcissistic individuals when you have no choice, such as in a work environment.

What Is a Narcissist?

Narcissistic Personality Disorder (NPD) is a clinical diagnosis, but it's important to note that many people exhibit narcissistic behaviors without being formally diagnosed. A narcissist is someone primarily driven by ego and lacking empathy. To better understand this, imagine empathy and ego as two ends of a spectrum:

- **Empathy** fosters deeper connection, understanding, and mutual growth.
- **Ego** is focused on self-interest, managing appearances, and controlling others.

Most people are somewhere in the middle, balancing empathy and ego. However, narcissistic individuals are stuck on the ego end of the spectrum, making authentic connections almost impossible. This lack of empathy makes it incredibly challenging to form healthy relationships with them.

When reflecting on my past marriages and former bosses, I now see the narcissistic traits clearly. At the time, though, I blamed myself for the issues in those relationships.

If your experience is anything like mine, by the time you realize the other person lacks empathy, you've already become deeply entangled in the relationship. You're emotionally invested and committed, making it harder to break free. Instead of recognizing their narcissistic tendencies, you might be more inclined to blame yourself for the tension, rather than consider that their behavior could be part of a larger pattern.

Can You Have Empathy for a Narcissist?

Some well-intentioned people may suggest that we should show empathy for narcissists. However, this advice can be controversial and even triggering for survivors of emotional abuse at the hands of a narcissist. The reaction from many who have been mistreated is often anger and resentment, not empathy.

Remember our discussion in Chapter 19 about breaking free from the past? We explored how our thoughts and emotions shape our beliefs, and how those beliefs influence the type of relationships we attract. If we cling to past patterns of emotional abuse, we risk repeating them. This is where empathy comes into play: it's a tool to reframe the past, especially when we've been victims of narcissistic abuse. But how do you summon empathy for someone who has emotionally harmed you?

The Roots of Narcissism: Childhood Trauma

Empathy doesn't mean excusing a narcissist's actions. This is a crucial point to understand. To develop a deeper sense of empathy for a narcissist, it helps to understand the origins of their behavior. Narcissism often stems from childhood trauma.

Research suggests that children who develop narcissistic traits typically experience severe emotional trauma between the ages of 4 and 6. This early trauma disrupts their ability to form empathy. Instead, they learn to:

- Mimic empathetic behavior as a survival tactic.
- Build elaborate facades to protect their fragile ego.
- Seek constant external validation and achievement.
- Develop sophisticated manipulation techniques to control their environment.

Imagine experiencing such trauma at a young age that it robs you of the ability to feel empathy. It's a heartbreaking reality for many narcissists. Understanding this doesn't excuse their harmful actions, but it helps us view their behavior with clarity instead of confusion.

Why Narcissism Is Hard to Detect

The challenge with identifying narcissism is that narcissists are often skilled at mimicking empathy. They can present a charming, empathetic façade because they've learned how to behave in ways that appear caring, even though they don't feel empathy. This ability to "fake it" comes from their childhood experiences, where they learned to protect their ego and survive emotionally. They learned that appearing empathetic could help them gain approval and avoid further harm.

By the time these individuals become adults, they are so adept at faking empathy and seducing people with their charm that it becomes easy to be sucked into their web. Like a Venus flytrap, narcissists can draw you in with their seemingly genuine behavior, only for you to realize too late that you've been trapped.

Understanding this is an important step in healing. It allows us to feel empathy—not for the narcissist's harmful actions—but for the child they once were, who never learned how to ask for help and had to cope by building a false self. While this doesn't excuse their behavior, we can recognize the pain they've experienced and have compassion for the trauma they went through.

Healing From Narcissistic Relationships

Once we understand that narcissism is a result of deep childhood trauma, we can begin to heal. We can replace feelings of anger and resentment with love and forgiveness—not for their actions, but for their experiences. We can also forgive ourselves for tolerating toxic behavior and feeling guilty for being manipulated.

Empathy becomes a powerful tool for self-healing. It allows us to move forward, free from the guilt and shame of staying in unhealthy relationships for too long. By practicing empathy and using the tools we've learned (such as self-regulation from Chapter 19), we can break free from the emotional weight of narcissistic abuse.

This shift in mindset empowers us to not only heal but grow. It helps us thrive in future relationships, using the wisdom gained from our experiences to create healthier, more fulfilling connections.

Recognizing Narcissistic Patterns

Perhaps you work with a narcissist and cannot easily change jobs for various reasons. Or maybe you're married to a narcissist with children involved, and leaving would have major consequences for everyone. How do you handle a relationship with a narcissist? First, it's crucial to understand their tactics. Second, recognize how their ego shapes their perspective—or, as I call it, their ego filter. Third, implement the 3 C's: Curiosity, Clarity, and Courtesy.

Common Narcissistic Tactics

Narcissists typically employ three main techniques to manipulate and control:

1. Love Bombing
- Overwhelming attention and affection
- Creating quick, intense emotional bonds
- Setting the stage for future emotional leverage

2. Gaslighting
- Manipulating your perception of reality
- Making you doubt your judgment and erode your self-trust
- Twisting facts to make you feel confused or crazy

3. Blame Shifting
- Refusing to accept responsibility for their actions
- Playing the victim
- Projecting their faults and mistakes onto others

Narcissists will often disregard your boundaries, pushing you to accept their behavior. Recognizing these patterns is essential because they bypass our usual defenses by exploiting our empathetic nature.

The Ego Filter

Narcissists filter everything through their ego. Think of their ego as a lens through which all communication passes. Every interaction is scrutinized based on:

- How it affects their image or reputation
- What they gain or lose in the situation
- How it positions them relative to others

This filter explains why narcissists often struggle to take accountability for their actions, especially if it might make them appear weak or vulnerable. During a breakup, for instance, they will almost always play the victim, protecting their image. In a professional setting, they are quick to take credit for successes but never admit to failures.

This ego filter is why traditional communication approaches often fail with narcissists. Once you understand this filter, you can adapt your communication strategy and implement the 3 C's.

Applying P.A.C.T. and the 3 C's with Narcissists

We've covered some core frameworks in this book, so here's how to thoughtfully adapt them specifically for navigating narcissistic relationships:

Purpose
- Focus on shared objectives rather than emotional connection.
- Frame suggestions in terms of mutual benefit.
- Emphasize their role in achieving positive outcomes.

Authenticity
- Maintain boundaries to avoid emotional entanglement.
- Present your competence without threatening their status.
- Build rapport, but avoid being emotionally vulnerable.

Communication (The 3 C's)

1. Curiosity
- Ask questions that allow them to showcase their expertise.
- Show genuine interest in their perspective.
- Avoid direct questions that challenge their self-image or provoke defensiveness.

2. Clarity

- Be specific and concrete in your communication.
- Document important conversations or agreements.
- Maintain clear and firm boundaries to protect yourself.

3. Courtesy

- Navigate carefully around ego triggers.
- Acknowledge their contributions, even if they seem minimal.
- Present criticism indirectly and with tact to avoid setting off their defensive mechanisms.

When dealing with narcissists, curiosity can be a great entry point for conversations. Asking about their opinion or expertise—without challenging their self-image—helps to engage them in a way that feeds their ego, which makes them more willing to interact. Clarity comes next: By asking for specific details or confirming your understanding, you foster trust and make it easier to communicate with them.

The third C, courtesy, is the most critical when it comes to narcissists. What offends them most? Anything that feels like an attack on their ego. Whether it's disagreeing with their opinion, resisting their feedback, or anything that threatens their image, narcissists can react strongly. Therefore, it's essential to approach these interactions with sensitivity and care.

Strategic Choices: Stay or Go?

You might be thinking, *"I don't want to sacrifice who I am just to appease a narcissist."* And that is a completely valid concern. In most situations, you shouldn't have to make such a sacrifice. However, narcissists rarely change. The chances of helping them improve are slim because they lack the capacity for empathy. They would need professional help, but admitting to needing help would threaten their ego—something most narcissists are unwilling to do.

At this point, you have to make a decision about what's most important to you right now.

In a Professional Relationship:
- Can you create enough emotional distance to maintain objectivity and function effectively?
- Do the benefits of the relationship truly outweigh the emotional cost?
- Are there ways to minimize direct interaction?

In a Personal Relationship:
- Is the relationship sustainable long-term?
- Are there children or other significant factors to consider?
- Do you have support systems in place to help you?

Ask yourself: Is staying in this relationship—whether for the kids, love, or a paycheck—still worth it? If it no longer feels worth it, consider seeking the guidance of a therapist to help you explore your options. Whether you choose to stay or leave, developing empathy for the narcissist can help you avoid falling into similar patterns with future narcissistic individuals. Ultimately, this will empower you to recognize your worth and protect your emotional well-being.

KEY TAKEAWAYS

Whether you stay or leave a relationship with a narcissist, understanding these dynamics will help you:
- Maintain emotional balance by detaching from their manipulative tactics.
- Protect your sense of self by setting and consistently sticking to clear boundaries.

- Make clearer decisions about your boundaries and your emotional well-being.
- Build healthier future relationships by recognizing and avoiding narcissistic patterns.

And always remember:

- Your worth isn't defined by how someone else treats you.
- Setting boundaries is not selfish—it's essential for maintaining your well-being.
- Seeking professional help is a sign of wisdom, not weakness.

It is my sincere hope that this book helps you avoid the struggles I endured: two marriages to partners who seemed to prioritized their egos over mutual growth and understanding. I wish for you to achieve the clarity I found much sooner.

Your empathy is a strength, not a weakness. The world needs more empathetic people who can create meaningful connections and bring out the best in others. By recognizing narcissistic patterns and adapting your communication strategies, you can protect yourself and stay true to who you are.

For further reading and an even more in-depth exploration of how to handle relationships with narcissists, I highly recommend the book, *It's Not You: Identifying and Healing From Narcissistic People,* by Dr. Ramani Durvasula.

22

The Art of First Impressions

Have you ever had one of those moments when you're mid-conversation and someone unexpectedly interrupts? It happened to me, and it turned into a great teaching point about communication. Let me set the scene.

I was at the studio, deep in a conversation with Aliyah, one of the incredible folks who helps run the facility. We were deep in conversation, discussing how our work could positively impact others. Then, out of nowhere, a guy walked up, all smiles, holding a bag of food. He apologized for interrupting and introduced himself—a bold move, right?

But here's where things went sideways. Instead of engaging with our discussion or showing curiosity, he made assumptions. He assumed we were part of a nearby group and that his interruption wasn't a big deal.

Aliyah and I remained polite, but there was an unspoken vibe: "How long is this going to last?" The lesson was clear—had he led with curiosity, asking about our conversation or how he could contribute, he would have left a much stronger first impression.

This moment perfectly illustrates why the 3 C's are essential for making great first impressions. Let's explore how to apply them to first impressions in both professional and personal settings.

The 3 C's of First Impressions

1. Lead with Curiosity

Remember our interrupting friend? His approach highlighted what happens when curiosity is overlooked. Now, imagine if he had:

- Noticed the engaged conversation
- Waited for a natural pause
- Asked, "I'm sorry to interrupt, but you both seem so engaged. What are you discussing?"

The difference is dramatic and would have yielded better results. When you lead with curiosity:

- You show respect for others' time and space
- You demonstrate emotional intelligence
- You create natural openings for connection

Here are some thoughtful questions that go beyond the usual "How are you?" and "What do you do?"—helping to spark deeper engagement and genuine connection in any setting.

In Professional Settings:
- "What brings you to this conference?"
- "What aspects of your work do you find most exciting?"
- "How did you get started in your field?"

On First Dates and Social Events:
- "What sparked your interest in [shared interest]?"
- "What's the story behind choosing your career path?"
- "What makes you light up when you talk about it?"

For Conflict Resolution:
- "Can you help me understand what you meant by that?"
- "What matters most to you in this situation?"
- "How can we both get what we want?"

2. Create Clarity
Clarity in first impressions means being intentional about:
- Your purpose for connecting
- The value you bring to the interaction
- Your respect for the other person's time

Here's what this might look like in a few different settings:

Professional Example:
"Hi, I'm Sarah. I noticed you're also in marketing tech. I'd love to hear your thoughts on [specific topic] if you have a moment."

Dating Example:
"I enjoyed hearing about your travel experiences. Would you be interested in continuing this conversation over coffee sometime?"

3. Show Courtesy
Courtesy goes beyond basic manners. It's about:

- Reading social cues
- Respecting boundaries
- Showing genuine appreciation

Here's how you might apply that in the following settings:

Professional Settings:
- Notice when someone is busy
- Offer to reconnect at a better time
- Follow up as promised

Dating Context:
- Respect personal space
- Listen more than you speak
- Express genuine appreciation for shared time

First Impression of Trey

The first time I met Trey, he captivated a crowd. He is charming, enthusiastic, and magnetic, and I didn't like him…at first. What was getting in the way of me being able to like Trey's clear stellar first impression to a crowd of people? My own ego.

At the time, Trey and I worked together at a fitness studio where I had built a strong reputation. I took pride in how I connected with clients and the trust I had earned. I didn't realize that I had allowed that reputation to affect my ego the way it did until Trey arrived. Instantly people were drawn to him. My ego interpreted his strong first impression as competition and a threat to the reputation I had built rather than an opportunity to connect.

But here's what changed: I chose curiosity over insecurity. By pausing to reflect on my jealousy, I realized Trey wasn't diminishing me; he was simply excelling. Instead of resisting, I saw an opportunity to learn. That mindset shift strengthened our friendship (we even stood in each other's weddings) and refined my communication approach.

When someone makes a strong impression, you don't have to let ego block your ability to learn from or connect with them. If you feel competitive or insecure, you can check your ego by:

- Leading with curiosity rather than judgment
- Being honest with yourself about what you feel and seek to understand why

Once I took these two steps, I recognized that my ego was blocking me from learning from a great coach. I'm grateful I chose curiosity over insecurity as quickly as I did. If you ever find yourself in a similar situation, appreciate the chance to practice Attractive Communication. You may just change a rivalry into a real friendship.

Reading the Room

Developing your ability to "read the room" is very helpful for creating positive first impressions. Look for:

Green Lights:
- ☑ Open body language
- ☑ Eye contact and smiles
- ☑ Engaged responses
- ☑ Reciprocal questions

Red Lights:
- ☒ Closed body language
- ☒ Short, dismissive responses
- ☒ Lack of eye contact
- ☒ Physical turning away

Recovery Strategies

Even the best communicators sometimes misread situations when making a first impression. When this happens:

1. Acknowledge the Mistake
- "I realize I may have interrupted something important."
- "I realize I may have come across as scatterbrained when we first met."

2. Offer an Exit
- "Please don't let me keep you if you're in the middle of something right now."
- "I hope we can have a do-over when I'm not so wound up from work stress and I'm more my authentic self."

3. Create Future Opportunity
- "Perhaps we could connect at a better time?"
- "Perhaps I can connect with you for a few minutes after next week's yoga class."

The First 30 Seconds Rule

Research shows that people form lasting impressions in the first 30 seconds. How can you make those seconds count? It's all about how you start. Let's take a look at an encounter I had with Ben.

My friend Ben, a real estate agent, and I were meeting for lunch. Ben is excitable and enthusiastic about life. When you ask him, "How are you?" He doesn't just reply; he shares a story. It might sound ordinary, if told by someone else, but his excitement makes it feel amazing. Ben knows how to make a great first impression in those first 30 seconds.

I used to think his impressions were solely due to his natural enthusiasm and personality. Then, I realized he was following a principle that goes beyond just being energetic: leading with curiosity—but not in the way you might think.

Ben applies this principle in a unique way, one that Charlie Houpert, co-founder of Charisma On Command and author of *Charisma On Command: Inspire, Impress, and Energize Everyone You Meet*, explains perfectly. He encourages us to "Start First." But what does that mean?

To "Start First" means to be bold enough to be the first to share something genuinely interesting or exciting that's happened to you. When you do this, you indirectly send a message to others that it's safe to do the same. This approach fosters a sense of openness and trust.

The beauty of leading with curiosity this way is that it makes you come across as both fun and trustworthy. It creates an environment where people feel more comfortable sharing their own thoughts and experiences, and naturally, they become more curious about yours.

Sounds obvious, right? Yet, the majority of people don't do this. Think about the most common responses to casual pleasantries like "How are you?" or "How's it going?" We usually say things like "I'm fine," "I've been so busy," or "Just hanging in there." Then we often just repeat the question back. "How about you?"

And what's the typical response to that? "I'm fine." From there, the conversation can easily slip into awkward silence or dull small talk about the weather or sports. So, let me ask—who really started first in that scenario? No one did.

Now, imagine the next time someone asks, "How are you?" Instead of offering a generic response, you Start First and share a brief, exciting story about the best part of your day. This sparks curiosity in others, invites them to open up, and makes you appear more charismatic, fun, and trustworthy. That's what Ben does so effortlessly, and it's a big reason people enjoy being around him and want to work with him.

You might be thinking, "But I don't have Ben's personality." The good news? You don't need to. People with all types of personalities have successfully applied the Start First principle to create more meaningful and engaging conversations.

Perhaps you're also wondering, "But I don't have anything exciting or interesting to share." Let me challenge that thought with one question: is there really nothing recently that made you smile or intrigued you? The Start First principle works even with simple things—whether it's sharing an insightful podcast, describing how a sandwich satisfied a craving, or talking about the joy of a delicious cup of coffee. It can be anything, as long as it sparks genuine excitement.

Here's a real example of how I used the Start First technique.

One day, before a fitness class, a client asked me the usual, "How's your day?" Instead of replying with a generic "Good" or "Fine," I decided to Start First and share something that genuinely interested me.

"I had the best Reuben sandwich I've had in a long time—from this hole-in-the-wall spot I didn't even know existed!" I said. "I was craving a good sandwich, so I searched on Google and found this hidden gem. It was delicious! What's been the best part of your day?"

Her response wasn't the typical, routine answer to small talk. Instead, she lit up and shared something she was excited about. Our conversation naturally flowed into a discussion about food, favorite restaurants, and hidden local gems. Starting First instantly turned a standard exchange into an engaging and memorable conversation.

The beauty of this technique? Your story doesn't need to be long or elaborate—just 30 seconds or less. In fact, keeping it short makes it even more effective.

For example, instead of a generic response to *"How are you?"*, you could say:

"I had a rough time getting up this morning because my neighbor's dog kept barking all night. But after making my favorite cup of coffee, I'm surprising myself with how productive I've been! What's been the best part of your day so far?"

Even a simple, everyday moment—like discovering a great sandwich or bouncing back from a rough morning—can create a meaningful connection. The key is to share what genuinely excites you. You don't need an exotic travel story; you just need authentic enthusiasm. That's what sparks conversations and builds connections in daily life.

In addition to "Start First," here are some other strategies to make the most of the first 30 seconds when making a first impression:

1. Start Strong
- Convey a warm smile
- Display confident posture (i.e. maintain an upright posture with your shoulders relaxed and back straight. Stand or sit tall, avoiding slouching, to convey confidence and assurance.)
- Speak in a clear voice
- Use open and expressive hand gestures

2. Show Interest
- Summarize and label what others say (see Part Three of this book to revisit summaries and labels)
- Use engaging and open body language, such as, a warm handshake, nodding, and good eye contact
- Ask relevant questions

3. Create Connection
- Mix supplicative and neutral vocal tones
- Acknowledge shared interests
- Build rapport naturally through genuine curiosity and establishing common ground

Cultural Considerations

Remember that first impression norms vary across cultures, so you must be flexible, open-minded, and respectful of cultural differences. Consider that:

- Eye contact expectations differ
- Personal space varies (4–12 ft is typically comfortable)
- Greeting customs change
- Conversation topics may be taboo

KEY TAKEAWAYS

Every first impression is an opportunity to create a meaningful connection. Whether in professional settings, social interactions, or dating, keep these principles in mind:

- **Start First** – Lead with genuine curiosity and share something interesting.
- **Set Clear Intentions** – Approach interactions with purpose and authenticity.
- **Show Respect** – Be courteous, considerate, and mindful of others' comfort.
- **Read and Respond to Social Cues** – Adapt to the energy and engagement of the conversation.
- **Recover Gracefully** – If a moment feels awkward, handle it with ease and confidence.

Above all, stay authentic while respecting others' space and energy. The best first impressions stem from a sincere interest in others, balanced with an awareness of their boundaries.

23

Influential Leadership: Stand Out in Your Career

T hink back to Cara's story from Chapter 2. She believed I deserved my promotion because I took the time to genuinely connect with people. She wasn't alone—clients and colleagues noticed it too.

Influential leadership isn't just about being friendly; it's about building authentic relationships that inspire others to go beyond the bare minimum and give their best effort.

This same principle has been key to my success as a fitness coach, and it can elevate your leadership presence in any profession. Now, let's explore how applying the P.A.C.T. principles and the 3 C's can help you stand out as a leader—regardless of your official title.

Beyond Authority: The Power of True Leadership Influence

Consider two team leaders at a software company:

Maria runs her team with clear expectations and regular rewards. Tasks get completed, but rarely exceed expectations. Her team does what's required, but seldom takes initiative beyond their assigned roles.

Then there's James. His team consistently delivers outstanding results and frequently suggests innovative solutions—without being asked. When asked what drives them, team members say, *"James believes in us. We don't want to let him down."*

The difference? James has mastered what I call Influential Leadership—the ability to inspire intrinsic motivation through genuine connection. Let's explore how you can develop this game-changing skill.

Purpose: Connect With What Drives People

Remember Sam and Alex's story from Chapters 2-5? Their shared purpose transformed a casual lunch conversation into a powerful partnership. Great leaders do the same—they take the time to understand what truly motivates each team member:

- What excites them about their work?
- What are their career aspirations?
- How do they want to grow?
- What impact do they want to make?

By aligning individual purposes with team goals, you create intrinsic motivation—the kind that no reward system can replicate.

Practical Application:
How to Apply This in Your Workplace or Home

1. Have regular "purpose conversations" with team members.
2. Connect daily tasks to larger, meaningful goals.
3. Create opportunities that align with individual aspirations.
4. Celebrate progress when others move closer to their purpose.

Authenticity: Build Trust Through Character

Leadership, authenticity, and influence about understanding others' motivations—it's about demonstrating the kind of character that earns trust and inspires others to follow you. Here are some ways you can do that:

- Show genuine interest in others' success
- Maintain composure under pressure
- Follow through on commitments
- Share credit for wins and take responsibility for setbacks
- Display both warmth and competence
- Lead by example—be the standard you want your team to follow
- Publicly acknowledge contributions
- Share learning experiences and vulnerabilities appropriately

Authentic leadership isn't about perfection—it's about consistency, integrity, and commitment to the people you lead.

Communication: Master The 3 C's

Many leaders fall short because they focus more on giving directives than on building meaningful connections. By emphasizing strict compliance with policies and procedures, interactions can feel cold and transactional. This stifles autonomy and diminishes an individual's sense of contribution. Now, let's explore the 3 C's—a framework that can transform leadership communication and foster meaningful connections:

1. Curiosity

Instead of saying, *"Here's what we need to do…"*, try leading with, *"What are your thoughts on this challenge?"*

To lead with curiosity:
- Ask open-ended questions about work processes
- Show genuine interest in team members' perspectives
- Seek to understand before offering solutions
- Create space for new ideas

2. Clarity

Instead of vague praise like, *"Good job,"* give specific, meaningful feedback: *"Your analysis of the customer data revealed insights that helped us adjust our strategy effectively."*

To lead with clarity:
- Set clear expectations
- Provide specific, actionable feedback
- Ensure shared understanding of goals
- Communicate the "why" behind decisions

3. Courtesy

Instead of rushing through interactions, demonstrate respect for others' time and contributions.

To lead with courtesy:
- Schedule conversations when you can be fully present
- Follow up on discussions and commitments
- Express genuine appreciation
- Respect work-life boundaries

Trust: The Foundation of Influence

Review the 3 Elements Of Trust in Chapter 6. When you consistently apply these principles—along with Attractive Communication that fosters deep connection—you build the kind of trust that encourages people to:

- Bring problems to you early
- Share innovative ideas
- Take calculated risks
- Go beyond minimum requirements
- Support team goals enthusiastically

Building Trust Through Actions

Trust isn't built through words alone—it's proven through action. Here's how you can demonstrate trustworthiness:

- Maintain confidentiality
- Stand up for your team
- Provide resources and support
- Remove obstacles to success
- Keep your word consistently

The Ripple Effect of Influential Leadership

As you apply these leadership principles, you'll begin to see a ripple effect that leads to:

- Increased voluntary participation
- Higher-quality work
- More innovative solutions
- Stronger team cohesion
- Better conflict resolution
- Improved retention
- Natural career advancement opportunities

We've explored how to apply influential leadership whether you're in a leadership role now or aspiring to be in one. The next step is career advancement. Let's explore how P.A.C.T. and the 3 C's can help you take that step.

Career Advancement Through Leadership

Here's what most people overlook about career advancement: **Technical skills get you in the door, but leadership influence gets you promoted.**

When you master P.A.C.T. and the 3 C's:

- Your teams consistently outperform expectations
- People actively want to work with you
- Word of your leadership spreads
- New opportunities come naturally

Think back to Cara's story. She recognized that genuine connection and the ability to bring out the best in others define great leadership. My promotion followed naturally because organizations need leaders who inspire excellence.

KEY TAKEAWAYS

As you strengthen your leadership influence:

1. Practice the 3 C's in every interaction
2. Align individual and team purposes to inspire motivation
3. Build trust through consistent character and follow-through
4. Focus on creating genuine connections—leadership is about people, not just authority

Remember: True leadership isn't about having power—it's about inspiring others to be their best. When you master the

P.A.C.T. principles, career growth becomes a natural outcome of your positive impact.

In the next chapter, we'll explore how to choose relationships wisely, ensuring your personal connections are as fulfilling as your professional ones.

PART SEVEN

Your Relationship Transformation

This final section is your roadmap to intentional, meaningful, personal connections. Here, you'll learn how to choose relationships wisely, understand the natural seasons of connection, and create a life rich with supportive, growth-oriented relationships. These chapters are about more than just maintaining connections— they focus on cultivating a network of relationships that energize, challenge, and celebrate you. You'll emerge with the skills to not just survive in relationships but to truly thrive.

Choose Your
Relationships Wisely

When it comes to relationships, it's crucial to understand that not everyone will share your perspective on what makes relationships work. Not everyone will have the same communication skills, emotional awareness, or willingness to grow. That's why it's up to you to decide who to form—or end—a P.A.C.T. with.

Think back to my story from the introduction. At that point in my life, everything had crumbled. I was suicidal, isolated, stuck in a job I hated, and, at my lowest moment, I even faced a gun pointed at me in public. The relationships I had chosen weren't supporting me—they were draining me. That's when I learned one of the hardest truths about relationships:

When any of the P.A.C.T. principles fail, the relationship becomes toxic.

But here's what changed everything: I started evaluating which relationships fueled me and which ones drained me. I took a hard look at the choices I had made. My first step? Turning to the most important relationship in my life—my wife, my supposed life partner. But when she refused to support me in finding help, the truth became clear: I needed to make different choices about all my relationships.

Here's what I learned:

Just because a P.A.C.T. ends doesn't mean it was a mistake to form in the first place. Some relationships are meant only for a season—and that's okay. We can be grateful for what they taught us. Ending a relationship doesn't mean the other person is bad or wrong. And if someone chooses not to form a P.A.C.T. with you, it doesn't mean you are unworthy of love, success, or happiness.

This is a truth many of us must face. Take Michelle, for example. In the next story, she finds herself confronting a similar realization...

The Power of Choice

Rain drummed steadily against the coffee shop windows as Michelle stared into her untouched latte, her reflection distorted in the cooling liquid. Across the table, her longtime friend Rachel fidgeted with her phone, barely making eye contact. The silence between them felt heavier than the gray clouds outside.

"I just don't understand," Michelle finally said, her voice barely above a whisper. "We used to tell each other everything. Now it feels like we're strangers who happen to meet for coffee once a month."

Rachel's fingers stilled on her phone, but her eyes remained fixed on the screen. "Things change, Michelle. People change."

The weight of unspoken words hung between them, a testament to a friendship that had slowly drifted from deep connection to superficial interaction. Michelle had spent months trying to rebuild their bond, applying everything she knew about communication and connection. Yet with each attempt, she felt the distance growing.

This scene plays out in countless variations across relationships every day. We invest time, energy, and emotional resources into connections that may no longer serve our growth or well-being.

The hardest truth about relationships isn't that they can end—it's that sometimes they should. I learned this firsthand through two failed marriages and several lost friendships. While painful at the time, those endings taught me a crucial lesson: **relationships that don't uphold all principles of P.A.C.T. inevitably turn toxic.** Accepting this truth is essential for maintaining healthy boundaries and fostering meaningful connections.

Understanding Relationship Seasons

Just as nature moves through seasons, relationships follow their own natural cycles. Some are meant to last a lifetime, while others serve a purpose for a specific season of our lives.

Consider the story of James and his mentor, Dr. Chen:

The university hallway buzzed with afternoon activity as James knocked on Dr. Chen's office door one last time. For three years, this modest office had been his sanctuary, a place where his academic dreams took shape under Dr. Chen's guidance. Now, with graduation approaching, both knew their relationship would change.

Dr. Chen looked up from his desk, his kind eyes crinkling at the corners. "Ah, James. Come in." He gestured to the familiar chair across from his desk, the same one where James had sat through countless discussions about research methodology and career aspirations.

"I'm not sure how to say goodbye," James admitted, his voice thick with emotion.

Dr. Chen smiled gently. "Who says we have to? Our relationship isn't ending, James. It's evolving. You're no longer my student, but that doesn't diminish what we've shared or what lies ahead. It just means our connection will take a different form."

This wisdom applies to all relationships. Some connections:

- Teach us valuable lessons
- Guide us through particular challenges
- Support us during crucial transitions
- Challenge our perspectives
- Facilitate personal growth

Understanding this natural ebb and flow allows us to appreciate relationships for what they bring into our lives—without forcing them to fit a mold they've outgrown.

The P.A.C.T. Assessment Framework

When evaluating relationships, consider how they align with the P.A.C.T. principles by asking yourself the following questions:

Purpose Alignment:
- Do we share compatible values and goals?
- Does this relationship support my growth?
- Are we moving in complementary directions?
- Does our connection meaningfully serve the purpose of each person involved?

Authentic Reciprocity:
- Is there mutual respect and admiration?
- Do we bring out the best in each other?
- Do we share and display common values?
- Do we naturally want to invest in the relationship?

Communication Quality:
- Can we have honest, open discussions?
- Do we practice the 3 C's (Curiosity, Clarity, Courtesy)?
- Is there genuine understanding and validation?
- Do we resolve conflicts constructively?

Trust Foundation:
- Is there consistent reliability and follow-through?
- Do we feel emotionally safe with each other?
- Is there mutual support during challenges?
- Can we be vulnerable without fear of judgment?

Recognizing When to Let Go

Stephanie sat in her car outside her best friend Jessica's house, hands gripping the wheel though the engine had cooled. Through the windshield, she saw Jessica's silhouette behind the curtains—unaware she was there. They hadn't spoken in weeks, not since their last argument, one of many that left them drained and distant.

The urge to knock, to try again, was strong. But as Stephanie watched the familiar shape move through the house, she realized: sometimes love means letting go.

Like Stephanie, we all face moments when we must reevaluate or release relationships that no longer serve us. Here are some key signs it may be time to let go:

1. Constant Energy Drain

If interactions consistently leave you exhausted, the relationship may be depleting rather than enriching. Signs include:

- A one-sided emotional investment where you're always the one giving.
- A need to tiptoe around conflicts to maintain peace.
- Feeling emotionally drained after every interaction rather than supported or uplifted.

2. Persistent Toxic Patterns

Some relationships fall into destructive cycles that erode trust and emotional well-being. These patterns include:

- Frequent judgment, criticism, or shame in communication.
- Repeated boundary violations that make you feel disrespected or unsafe.
- Undermining your personal growth rather than encouraging it.

3. Misaligned Values

As we grow, our values evolve—and sometimes, relationships don't evolve with us. Signs of misalignment include:

- Conflicting core beliefs that create ongoing tension.
- Diverging life paths that make it difficult to maintain a meaningful connection.
- A loss of mutual respect, leaving the relationship feeling forced rather than fulfilling.

4. Communication Breakdown

Communication breakdown represents the final stage of relationship deterioration. Healthy relationships thrive on open, honest dialogue. When communication falters, the relationship starts to deteriorate. Warning signs include:

- Conversations feeling superficial, emotionally guarded, or marked by frequent confrontation
- A lack of understanding or validation, leading to defensiveness and emotional shutdown.
- Conflict resolution becoming destructive instead of constructive, further fracturing the relationship.
- Emotional safety completely erodes, making authentic expression not just difficult, but dangerous.

The Art of Graceful Transition

When I prioritized healthy relationships, everything changed. My marriage ended, some friendships faded, and yet, other relationships strengthened in unexpected ways. The people who remained supported me through my darkest moments, offering space to heal without judgment. What did these relationships have in common? They followed the P.A.C.T. principles:

- **Purpose** – We served and supported each other's life goals.
- **Attraction** – We shared core values that naturally drew us together.
- **Communication** – We spoke openly and honestly, without shame or fear of judgment.
- **Trust** – We built and maintained a foundation of mutual respect and emotional reliability.

Ending or redefining a relationship doesn't have to be dramatic or hurtful. Here's how to transition with clarity and respect:

1. Use Clear Communication
When necessary, be honest but kind:
- Express gratitude for the shared experiences.
- Acknowledge the relationship's value, even if it's changing.
- Be transparent about your needs and boundaries.
- If appropriate, leave the door open for future reconnection.

2. Maintain Respect
Even as relationships shift, integrity matters:
- Avoid gossiping or speaking negatively about others.
- Honor past confidences, no matter how the relationship may have ended.
- Recognize how the relationship helped shape your personal growth.
- Wish the other person well, even if paths diverge.

Creating Space for New Connections

As some relationships naturally conclude or evolve, space opens for new, meaningful connections. This isn't about replacing old relationships—it's about aligning your social circle with your current path.

How to Cultivate New Relationships

- **Clarify your intentions** – Are you looking for friendships, mentors, or professional networks?
- **Engage in aligned environments** – Join groups, workshops, or social spaces that reflect your values.
- **Pursue shared interests** – Activities like fitness, travel, or creative hobbies often lead to natural connections.
- **Apply P.A.C.T. principles** – Set the foundation for healthy relationships from the start.

Practice Discernment

Not every new connection will be the right fit. Stay mindful by:

- Observing whether values align naturally.
- Recognizing early signs of toxicity or emotional drain.
- Trusting your gut—do certain people energize you or leave you uneasy?
- Allowing relationships to develop organically instead of forcing connections.

Maintaining Balance

- Don't rush to fill every void—let meaningful connections form naturally.
- Give relationships time to evolve before defining their role in your life.
- Honor existing relationships that continue to support and uplift you.
- Stay true to yourself rather than adjusting to fit someone else's expectations.

The Courage to Choose

Making conscious choices about relationships requires courage. It means facing uncomfortable truths, setting clear boundaries, accepting natural endings, embracing new beginnings, and trusting your judgment.

Remember Maya from our opening story? She eventually made peace with the evolution of her friendship with Rachel. Rather than forcing the connection to fit its old pattern, she acknowledged its season had passed. This acceptance let her focus on relationships that aligned with her journey while feeling grateful for what she and Rachel had shared.

KEY TAKEAWAYS

As you apply these principles to your own relationships, keep in mind:

- Every relationship teaches valuable lessons.
- Not all connections are meant to last forever.
- Choosing wisely honors both yourself and others.
- Growth sometimes requires letting go.
- New connections emerge when you create space for them.

Reflection Questions

Take a moment to consider:

1. Which relationships in your life consistently uplift and energize you?
2. Where do you notice patterns of toxicity or energy drain?

3. What relationships might need reassessment or boundaries?

4. How can you create space for connections that better serve your growth?

5. What lessons have your past relationships taught you about choosing wisely?

Choosing your relationships wisely isn't about exclusivity—it's about intention and authenticity. It's about creating space for relationships that support your growth while honoring the natural seasons of connection in your life.

25

The Joy of
Quality Connections

As I began to heal from my failed marriages and the loss of some friendships, other positive changes naturally unfolded. My relationships improved. Loyal friends cheered for my successes. My career soared, and I made new, empowering connections. Looking back, the contrast between my past and present is striking. The relationships that energized and supported me all followed the P.A.C.T. principles. When my relationships thrived, so did every other area of my life. This mirrors what the Harvard Study discovered after following participants for over 80 years: quality relationships are crucial for happiness, health, and longevity. Allow me to share a story that illustrates this truth.

The Power of Positive Relationships

The morning sun streamed through the windows of Rose's small bakery, casting warm light on two elderly women sharing coffee and fresh-baked scones. Maria and Sophie, both in their eighties, had been meeting here every Thursday morning for the past thirty years. Their laughter filled the space, drawing smiles from other customers who couldn't help but be touched by their obvious joy in each other's company.

"Do you remember when we first met?" Sophie asked, her eyes twinkling. "You were trying to wrangle those twin boys of yours at the park, and I just happened to have an extra juice box in my bag."

Maria chuckled, the sound rich with memory. "Those boys are grandfathers now, and here we are, still sharing our morning coffee. Who would have thought a chance meeting at a playground would lead to a friendship that's lasted half our lives?"

People with quality social connections live longer, maintain better mental health, and experience more joy in their daily lives. It's clear that positive relationships—like the one between Maria and Sophie—are essential to our well-being.

The Elements of Lasting Connections: Shared Purpose, Support, and Growth

Every quality relationship starts with something small. Virtually no relationship begins with an instant, deep connection. It typically begins with a shared interest and develops over time. Quality relationships aren't just about having someone to talk to—they're about having people who actively support your growth and well-being. Consider the story of the "Sunrise Six":

Every morning at 5:30 AM, six women gathered at the local park for their daily walk. They had started as strangers, each seeking to improve their health, but over the course of three years, they had become an indispensable part of each other's lives. They celebrated victories together—weight-loss goals met, promotions earned, and children's achievements. They supported each other through challenges—health scares, family conflicts, and personal losses.

When Linda struggled with depression after her divorce, the group adjusted their schedule to ensure someone could walk with her every day—not just during their regular meeting time. When Mei's mother was diagnosed with cancer, the others organized a meal rotation and helped with hospital visits. What made their connection special wasn't just the daily exercise—it was their genuine investment in each other's well-being.

Creating Your Own Success Story

These stories show that meaningful relationships help us grow, respect each other, and face challenges together. It's not about having many connections, but about having deep, supportive ones with a shared purpose. Letting go of toxic relationships might cause temporary sadness, but it paves the way for healthier connections that truly support your growth. Whether you choose to let go of certain relationships or work on strengthening the ones you have by applying the principles of P.A.C.T., you can foster growth in both your current and future connections.

To create lasting, positive relationships, try practicing these tips:

1. Invest Time Consistently
- Schedule regular meet-ups
- Create shared rituals
- Make relationship maintenance a priority
- Show up reliably for important moments

2. Practice Active Support
- Celebrate others' successes
- Offer practical help during challenges
- Listen without judgment
- Show up during difficult times

3. Foster Growth Together
- Share learning experiences
- Encourage personal development
- Support each other's goals
- Create collaborative projects

4. Maintain Open Communication
- Practice the 3 C's (Curiosity, Clarity, Courtesy)
- Address conflicts constructively
- Share feelings and experiences openly
- Keep building trust through honesty

 *KEY TAKEAWAYS*

Every quality relationship begins with a choice. Sometimes, that choice involves letting go, while other times it's about being open to new connections, as Maria was with Sophie that day in the park. As you reflect on the stories and strategies shared in this chapter, consider:

- Which relationships in your life embody these positive, uplifting qualities?
- How can you invest more intentionally in your key relationships and connections?
- What new connections might you cultivate?
- How can you be a more supportive friend, colleague, or family member?

Remember, every meaningful connection starts somewhere. Whether it was Maria and Sophie's chance meeting at the playground or the Sunrise Six's morning walks, each relationship began with someone taking the initiative to build something valuable.

Choosing relationships wisely isn't about being selective or exclusive for superficial reasons—it's about being intentional and authentic in your connections. It's about creating space for relationships that support your growth while honoring the natural seasons of connection in your life.

The P.A.C.T. principles aren't just theoretical; they form a proven foundation for building and maintaining relationships that energize you rather than drain you. As you move forward in choosing your P.A.C.T.s, let these timeless principles guide your decisions about who gets to be a part of your life story. Each step toward stronger relationships is an investment in your well-being and happiness.

Glossary

Attractive Communication: Demonstrating warmth and competence in communication that makes people feel acknowledged, understood, and validated

Clarity: The quality of being clear and easy to understand

Communication: The process of creating shared mental pictures through words, sounds, signs, and behaviors, to build trust, foster connection, and create positive influence.

Courtesy/Tact: The practice of avoiding unnecessary offense to others; showing consideration for how words and actions impact others

Curiosity: The desire to learn or know more about something or someone to understand better or discover something you did not know before

Empathy: The ability to understand and share the perspective and feelings of another

Goal: Powerful motivators that are temporary

Influence: The ability to affect someone's actions or attitude, often in an indirect way

Judgment: Labeling, or deciding that an action or motive of something, someone, or a group, is factually right, wrong, good, or bad.

Leadership: The ability to guide, influence, and motivate others to work together and achieve a common goal

Narcissism (NPD): A personality disorder caused by childhood trauma causing a lack of empathy and ego-driven behavior *(Please Note: When used in this book, our definition is limited to a non-clinical diagnosis of narcissistic tendencies.)*

P.A.C.T.: 1. A method of building and maintaining relationships through four essential elements: Purpose (shared values and goals), Authenticity (character-based qualities), Communication (clear and empathetic exchange), and Trust (mutual reliability and safety). 2. An agreement or alliance between people.

Purpose: A powerful motivator that comes from within and does not have an end to fulfillment

Relationship: Two or more people who relate to each other; being linked or associated together through something shared in common.

Shame: The feeling of being small, unworthy, flawed, and never "good enough."

Toxic Communication: Communication that unnecessarily evokes feelings of shame, judgment, and or selfishness.

Diagrams and Illustrations

Communication is seeing the same picture in our minds.

Miscommunication is not seeing the same picture in our minds.

Communication with Your Circle Of Trust

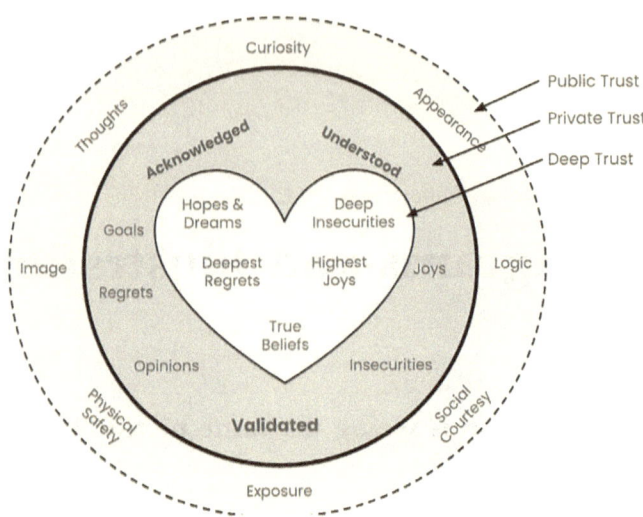

Attractive Communication (the left arrow) allows for deep trust and connection. Toxic Communication (the right) prevents connection.

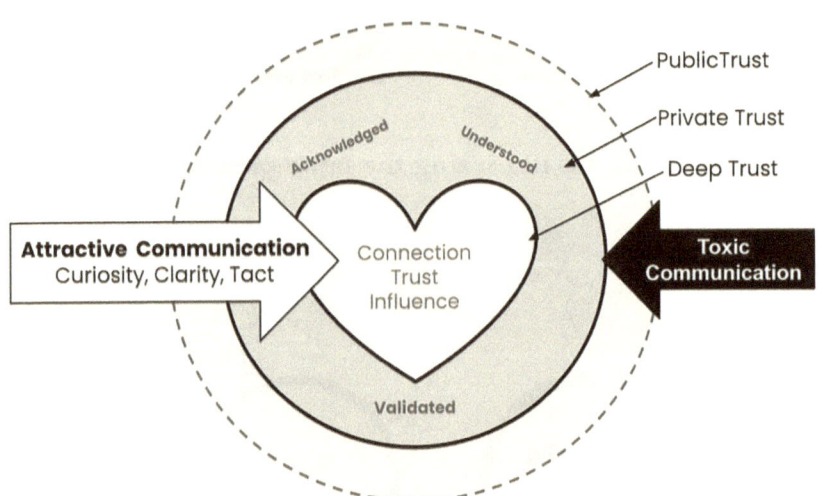

Attractive Communication demonstrates charisma, making you more likable and influential. Toxic Communication promotes shame, distrust, and apathy.

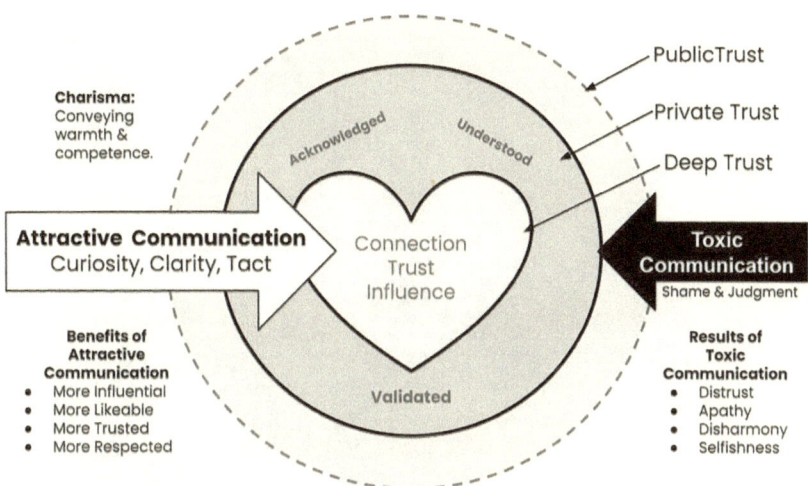

Communication is the bridge that connects you and others and builds strong bonds of trust.

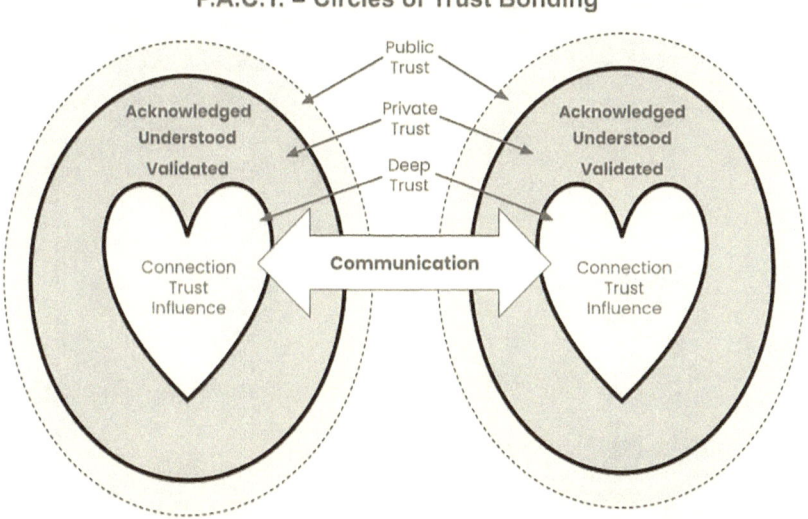

Recommended Reading

For in-depth understanding of purpose and how to find it:
Start With Why – Simon Sinek
Find Your Why – Simon Sinek

For in-depth understanding of body language and social cues:
Cues – Vanessa Van Edwards

For in-depth understanding of narcissism:
It's Not You – Dr. Ramani Durvasula

Other recommendations:
Nonviolent Communication – Marshall Rosenberg
Never Split the Difference – Chris Voss
Supercommunicators – Charles Duhigg
Trust – Dr. Henry Cloud
Daring Greatly – Brené Brown
Dare to Lead – Brené Brown

About the Author

Rico Armstrong Jr. has over two decades of public speaking experience and has coached and facilitated more than 6,500 group training sessions. As a passionate researcher of practical communication skills, he specializes in breaking down complex relationship and communication principles into simple, actionable frameworks. His debut book, *The Power of P.A.C.T. in Attracting Authentic Relationships: The Guide to Being Emotionally Safe, Connected, and Successful in Personal and Professional Relationships*, introduces the P.A.C.T. framework and the 3 C's of Communication—making effective communication accessible to anyone. When he's not exploring leadership and communication strategies, Rico enjoys cooking, traveling, and the musical arts.

@coachricoarmstrong

@coachricoarmstrong

AttractAndImpact.com

www.ingramcontent.com/pod-product-compliance
Lightning Source LLC
Chambersburg PA
CBHW021221130626
46554CB00004B/1314

* 9 7 9 8 9 9 9 8 6 1 0 7 0 7 *